UNDERDOGS

ALSO BY KEITH DEWHURST

PLAYS

Rafferty's Chant
Lark Rise to Candleford
War Plays (*Corunna!*, *The World Turned Upside Down*,
The Bomb in Brewery Street)
Don Quixote
Black Snow
Philoctetes (translation)

TELEVISION

'Running Milligan' in *Z Cars*, 'Last Bus' in *Scene*

NOVELS

Captain of the Sands
McSullivan's Beach

THEATRE MEMOIR

Impossible Plays (with Jack Shepherd)

FOOTBALL

When You Put on a Red Shirt:
Memories of Matt Busby, Jimmy Murphy and
Manchester United

Keith Dewhurst

Underdogs

The Unlikely Story of Football's First FA Cup Heroes

YELLOW JERSEY PRESS
LONDON

Published by Yellow Jersey Press 2012

2 4 6 8 10 9 7 5 3 1

First published in Great Britain in 2012 by
Yellow Jersey Press
Random House, 20 Vauxhall Bridge Road,
London SW1V 2SA

www.vintage-books.co.uk

Addresses for companies within The Random House Group Limited can be found at:
www.randomhouse.co.uk/offices.htm

The Random House Group Limited Reg. No. 954009

A CIP catalogue record for this book
is available from the British Library

ISBN 9780224083133

The Random House Group Limited supports The Forest Stewardship Council
(FSC®), the leading international forest certification organisation. Our books
carrying the FSC label are printed on FSC® certified paper. FSC is the only forest
certification scheme endorsed by the leading environmental organisations, including
Greenpeace. Our paper procurement policy can be found at
www.randomhouse.co.uk/environment

Typeset in Bembo by Palimpsest Book Production Limited
Falkirk, Stirlingshire
Printed and bound by CPI Group
(UK) Ltd, Croydon, CR0 4YY

In memory of our friend Banjo

Contents

PART TWO: Old Etonians

List of Illustrations

Preamble: Football Mania

From about ten thirty on the night of 29 January 1879, a party of twenty-one young people waited for thirty-five minutes on London's Aldersgate Street underground station (now called Barbican) for their connection to St Paul's, where they were booked into a private hotel. They had been travelling for more than eight hours from the Lancashire cotton town of Darwen, and most of them were millworkers, although one of the men may have been an Old Harrovian. Another was a doctor, and a third a junior accountant. A fourth was a journalist, and another may well have been James Christopher Ashton, a mill owner's son who fancied himself as a writer. There were certainly two Scotsmen, named Jimmy Love and Fergus Suter, and two women, one with a baby, whose names were not recorded. The mill lads were provincial, and joked to cover their unease. When one of them, whom the others nicknamed Jemmy o' Woods, asked for a cup of tea at the refreshment bar the waitress could not understand his accent, and thought that he was French. This caused louder hilarity, at which Londoners on the platform were not amused.

In such a fashion did the Darwen football team arrive in London, to play on the following afternoon their third round Football Association Cup tie against Remnants, a Berkshire club of moneyed, well-connected people. Darwen's victory was a sensation, football's first giant-killing, and one of the women with them paced the touchline saying, 'Fancy! A lot of working chaps beating a lot of gentlemen!'

Her words have echoed down the years because of what happened next: in the Cup quarter-finals Darwen were drawn against Old Etonians. They went again to Kennington Oval and with fifteen minutes to go were 5–1 down, blown away by physically superior opponents. In 1795 the people of Darwen had been called 'a tall, florid and comely race', but after three generations of industrialisation they were punier than their privileged adversaries. Then with a superior brand of play they fought back to achieve a draw, and it needed two replays to settle the issue.

Rulers against ruled, rich against poor, champions who used old football tactics against underdogs who used new, the men who were supposed to have invented the game against the lower orders who had taken it up: it was an encounter that even during the weeks of the replays was seen to be symbolic. And it had a subtext that within a year or two became a bitter controversy.

For all their gamesmanship, which shocked the newspapers at the time, Old Etonians were the flower of the gentlemen who played for the pleasure of having healthy minds in healthy bodies, whereas Darwen, for all their cash-strapped image, were the harbingers of the spectator sports future. Love and the inspirational Suter were paid professionals, the first men in the world of whom this can be said for certain, and the team itself was the first middle-class attempt to create a ruthless success machine: the first step on that lurid road to the San Siro, Old Trafford and the Nou Camp.

'Darwen has been affected by a kind of "Football Mania" and there happens to have been no life in the town, only that caused by football,' wrote the sparky journalist and eventual local newspaper tycoon J. J. Riley in 1879. Today the excitement is long gone and the little town is a run-down shadow of what it was. Mills and their chimneys have been demolished. Pubs have been shut down, and cut-price video shops boarded up. But one can still stand in the main street, as Fergus Suter did, and see moorland a few hundred yards away, and the question arises: why? Why did modern football begin here? What secret chains hold us to that past? What was it about Darwen that made it happen?

PART ONE

Darwen

Folk football

Darwen's inhabitants call it 'Darren', and themselves 'Darreners', and it is one of those places that despite everything has maintained a persistent sense of identity. Since Edward Heath's local government reforms of the 1970s it has been part of Blackburn, as it was for centuries. Yet for a glorious and hard-won period after 1878 it was its own borough, and had its own Member of Parliament, and the mid-Victorian drive to achieve this expressed itself also in the vainglorious ambitions of the football club. Both town and club were created by the Industrial Revolution, from what was a scattering of hamlets and smallholdings on a spur of the Pennine Moors. To the south are Bolton and Manchester, and Darwen is over the top, facing north, in the cleft down which the little River Darwent flows to Blackburn. In the eighteenth century the river was famous for salmon, and at the edge of Blackburn, where the Rovers' Ewood Park ground stands today, milch cows grazed, and the fields were white with cloths laid out to bleach.

Blackburn was Tory, Anglican and built of brick, but Darwen was built of stone, more radical in politics and Nonconformist in religion. The Walsh family, who when they were rich started the football club in

1872, were descended from a vicar of Blackburn who in 1606 was ejected from his living for Nonconformity and retreated to a moorland smallholding.

After the Civil Wars the political consensus that made England a constitutional monarchy had regarded such Protestant dissenters as unsafe left-wingers, and Roman Catholics as a menace from the right, and both were excluded from many powerful social positions by Acts of Parliament. These Acts were not fully repealed until the 1830s, and they created among the excluded feelings of difference and self-reliance. These were exaggerated in a place like Darwen, which was isolated and not on the way to anywhere: there was no proper road across the moors until 1797, and no railway until the late 1840s.

Darwen's people mixed subsistence farming with handloom weaving, and weavers were literate, suspicious of strangers and famously independent. John Duxbury, an old man born in Darwen in 1822 and interviewed by the *Blackburn Evening Telegraph* in 1906, said that 'handloom weavers never worked Monday, and sometimes they took Tuesday and Wednesday as well'. They had their own machines at home, and either walked to Blackburn with their finished lengths of cloth in sacks and brought back their yarn, 'twist' as it was called, or dealt with putters-out, who sent men round the district with pack ponies.

So long as the work was done weavers were masters of their time, and it was reckoned that Darwen had a footballing advantage over neighbouring villages because so many of the players were weavers who took time off to practise, and even played at night under a full moon.

Folk football had been played for centuries, all over the country, under all sorts of rules and conditions. As often as not it took place on Shrove Tuesday, because by medieval tradition that was the day on which apprentices had a holiday. Games were cheerfully violent and involved large numbers; and although the gentry were the backers of horse-racing, prize-fighting, cock-fighting and so forth, football was a mob event outside their interest and protection, which meant that it could be attacked and banned. Among schoolboys football never did die out, but by the end of the eighteenth century adult games were rare.

Evangelicals hated the drink and gambling that accompanied most sporting events, and the cruelty of many. And in the years of the French Revolution, and homegrown protests against economic change, magistrates were extremely suspicious of crowds. After all, what was football *for*, in a commercial world that scorned the superstition which underlay so many ancient customs?

'I cannot consider the game of football at all gentlemanly,' wrote an old Etonian named Henry Blake in 1833. 'It is a game which the common people of Yorkshire are particularly partial to.' In other words, football was not adult. Sport was not yet the shorthand for the entire philosophy of Britain's ruling class, and to play up, play up and play the game was not yet the code of a gentleman. Where football survived it did so in places like Ashbourne in

Derbyshire, the villages around Penistone in Yorkshire, and Darwen itself: insignificant upland locations which still had space in which to play. During John Duxbury's childhood there would have been old people in Darwen who remembered mob football of unlimited numbers that took place over a large area. One goal was positioned at Mouldon Water near Blackburn, and the other at Culshaw Bar on Bull Hill, an uphill distance across open country of some two miles. This football seems to have involved one district competing against another, men from Darwen against teams from as far away as Bury, and what ended it was not so much public disapproval as the effects of economic change: the industrialisation of the cotton trade.

Dirty Darren

Spinning machines were the first to be invented, and they were installed to begin with in water-driven mills. For this Darwen's river was perfect: it had a manageable flow, which even when it was in spate would not back up and halt the machinery, and low banks on which to build. The first mill was erected in 1775 by Thomas Eccles, a farmer-weaver whose land was on the water. His family married into that of John Shorrock, another yeoman, who built a mill in 1784. Shorrock's original partner was a Blackburn grocer and draper who had cash flow. To work the mill they imported pauper apprentices from London.

Such factories were not large, but they hugely increased both production and fluctuations in the trade cycle. In booms handloom weavers prospered, but once power looms had been invented they faced extinction. Power looms were suited to the district's coarse cloths, and could be worked by women and children. Men became redundant. John Duxbury's family owned six handlooms, but saw no future for him, and at the age of seven he was sent into Bowling Green Mill as a full-time throstle spinner. The mill worked six days a week from five in the morning to nine at night, but with meal breaks.

A throstle was an early spinning machine that whistled like a bird.

In the 1790s three incoming entrepreneur families had rented mills: the Greenways and the Potters, both of whom had paper-making and dye works interests around London, and that of Richard Hilton, who had won the contract to provide the Army with calico. Apart from these few, and partners acquired much later by the Potters, other people who became rich were local: riverside mill builders or families whose land had extractable stone, slate or coal. Because of a geological fault some of the coal was a mere twenty inches below the surface. Darwen may have been isolated but its industrialisation was self-powered. It was a close-knit place, and families who had been farmer-weaver neighbours for two centuries soon found themselves at the extremes of wealth and poverty.

Altogether, John Duxbury and John Chadwick, another old-timer, who was born in 1830 and also interviewed in 1906, give a vivid impression of these years in which the valley of smallholdings became the industrial town known as 'Dirty Darren' – 'brutal scenes' on its unpaved streets, water carried from the wells, sewage and industrial waste poured into the river, public houses open most of the night, footpads abroad, and illicit whisky stills on the moors. The old manorial court would meet in the Waggon and Horses inn, to appoint meaningless medieval officials like a Bellman and a Moss Looker, but had neither the money nor the powers to address the problems of industrialisation and wage slaves.

Not that spirits were extinguished. In the new magistrates' court working-class women shouted ribaldries at the bench, and a regular delinquent nicknamed Yellow Frock was famous for her spats with a lawyer from Blackburn, who because he was very thin was called 'Fat Dick'. As for sports, Duxbury and Chadwick witnessed horse-racing, dog-fighting, cock-fighting, bull-baiting and bear-baiting: a man brought a bear to Blacksnape, where an old Roman road cut across the moors east of Darwen, and locals paid a fee for their dogs to have a go at it. Duxbury saw a touring theatre run by a man named Swallow play *Maria Marten* and Shakespeare outdoors, on waste ground near factories; and there was still the football.

Thirteen a side

This football differed, however, from the game that within living memory had raged across miles of open country. By about 1820 moorland pastures had begun to be enclosed for more commercial farming, which sidelined the Moss Looker, who had rounded up stray animals. Old rights of way near new coal pits and quarries were allowed to lapse, and more factories were built along the river. The football spectacle shrank to a game of some thirty players a side in 'a good-sized meadow', where the object was to kick the ball over the fence at the opposing end.

Was this meadow the ancient Town Field, common land where the valley floor began to flatten? Maybe not. But in 1830, a year in which eighteen power looms were destroyed by rioters, one of them a woman who was transported to Australia, Darwen's last recorded folk football matches took place, not near the town itself but on the moors.

There were two games, the first of them on 'Collop Monday', the day before Shrove Tuesday, against a team from Tottington near Bury. Tottington and Darwen are about six miles apart and the game was played at Edgworth, a village three miles from each, in a triangular field facing the Round Barn public house.

The pitch was marked out with flags to make the playing area rectangular, and the landlord of the Round Barn held the £2 10s.-a-side stakes. The game ended in a dispute and the Darwen team walked off, took the stake money, and spent it in the nearby Grey Horse inn. Tottington objected and issued a £5-a-side challenge to a rematch, which was accepted.

This game took place a month later on another neutral ground at Turton, again on the moors, and was won by Darwen in front of what were reckoned to be 5,000 spectators. At this time the population of Darwen was about 6,000, and people must have been drawn from far and wide by the fact that Tottington had engaged, and presumably paid, the famous Ben Hart from Bolton. He was a weaver who had made a deal of money from side stakes and betting on himself in foot races, or pedestrianism, as it was called.

In both games there were thirteen a side, and crude notions of teamwork and positional play. Each side had five backs, two 'side' players, and six 'in' players plus a 'trundler-in'. Hart may be presumed to have been a side player, who hoped to use his speed when the ball came free. To start, the teams lined up shoulder to shoulder, facing each other and about two yards apart. A trundler-in then rolled the ball into the gap. The first team to score twice won, the ball having to be carried or kicked over the opposing end-line. After a goal, the trundler-in whose team had conceded restarted play. The Darwen players all wore white stockings, to be distinguishable from their opponents in the melee. The crowd drank, swore and laid bets, and at one point Tottington supporters threw pigeons into the air, as a signal to their men to attack. Players wore an iron clog on one foot and a shoe on the other, and are said to have wielded stones and sticks, and to have been lashed at by people in the crowd brandishing hammers and cleavers. There were broken noses, dislocated joints and gashed shins.

Francis Brindle, a spectator who had fought at Waterloo, said later that nothing in the battle was as bad as what he saw in that match.

'Talk about Russians and Bashi-Bazooks,' he said, 'they weren't in it!'

But it was the last big Darwen game, and the last big crowd, for almost fifty years.

Young lads in fustian

It is around 1830 that, according to the received history of football, the folk game disappeared. Football, it is said, was kept alive by the old public schools, each with its own rules, so that it was boys going home as adults who in the end returned it to ordinary people. Most public school boys lived around London, and when they continued to play football as grown-ups many of the clubs they founded reflected their positions in society: old boys, regimental, universities and government departments. These players were what history has called them, 'Gentlemen Amateurs', and as their clubs sought fixtures they realised that what was needed was a common and codified set of rules. This led to the formation of the Football Association in 1863, and the spread of the game thereafter.

This triumphal outline is true, but does little justice to the richness of the facts. For example: organised eleven-a-side football was indeed brought to the area around Darwen by local rich boys who had been sent to Harrow School, but the workers they enlisted to play already knew the game, if only at a low and scrappy boyhood level. In 1841 the historian John Graham visited Darwen and described how when the factory whistles blew at lunchtime dozens of young lads in fustian ran out to play football in the streets. Strictly speaking, the Highway Act of 1835 had made street games illegal, but no one seems to have taken much notice, and where else could they play? New Mill and its workers' cottages covered the Town Field; and it was not until 1863, when the town's rich men who had founded the cricket club in 1845 finally purchased a meadow at Barley Bank, that a large area was set aside for sport.

Despite this, and despite the fact that working hours were so long that in winter operatives went to the mill in darkness and returned in darkness, modern social historians have found newspaper evidence of matches in Bolton, Blackburn, Darwen, Rochdale, Manchester and Holmfirth well into the 1840s. They were organised by publicans, who put the notices in the papers and held the side stakes. The teams were of varying numbers. Ben Hart himself, who became landlord of the Sir Sidney Smith tavern, organised games in Bolton, one of them between men of the town and the local garrison. There is similar evidence that moorland pub games, usually with six men a side, were played around Penistone in Yorkshire into the 1850s.

If the record fades thereafter it is not necessarily because the game did, but because the tax on newspapers killed off many early local news-sheets. More modern papers did not appear until later. The weekly *Darwen News*, for example, was not founded until 1874. But where the game persisted, so did its emotions, and its appeal as a metaphor for heroic deeds. Consider this neo-classical verse:

> Here's a field for courage and glory
> High achievements the hero still grace
> What in real war now lives but in story
> Have found in its mimic a place.

Does this describe the emotions of Darwen versus Tottington, or of the men who came out of mills and foundries to keep the game alive in makeshift places, or even the world of the 1950s comic book hero Roy of the Rovers? It does indeed, but in fact it is part of a poem written in 1847 about football at Westminster School.

Footer

Over the decades Darwen weavers adapted folk football to the spaces in which they were able to play, and so did boys at Westminster, Eton, Harrow, Winchester, Charterhouse, Rugby and no doubt many forgotten institutions as well. The difference was that the public school boy had playing areas, abundant free time, and cash. Money to pay for sport was added to parents' bills, although it was the boys who decided how to spend it. Boys arranged the Eton and Harrow cricket match in 1805, when because of his lameness Lord Byron batted with a runner; afterwards the teams went to the Haymarket Theatre and created a disturbance, rather like Premiership footballers in a night club. Harrow boys engaged their first cricket professional in the 1820s, when cricket was king because its universal rules had been developed in the adult world and made it easy to find opponents.

Football was slower to mature, and there were many varieties, each particular to its school, and adapted like the Darwen games to specific landscapes and architecture, to old affections and to what soon became intense traditions. Winchester football, for example, was a medieval street game taken to a playing field, but, sooner than change the game they loved, the players reproduced the narrowness and restrictions of the original street. This unique event still exists but has had no influence on the wider football. Almost the same is true of Charterhouse, where football was played in the indoor cloister from the school's foundation in 1611 until its move to Godalming in Surrey in 1872.

At Eton, on football fields first mentioned in 1766, several informal matches would take place at the same time. Bigger boys played in the middle of the field and smaller boys nearer the wall. The more the various groups encroached on one another the more necessary it became to define the areas of play. This demarcation narrowed the space along the wall occupied by the smaller boys and two sets of rules emerged: one for the wall and its physical features and one for the field. Both were mature by the 1850s, and both survive: the Wall Game is a glorious fossil and the Field Game, although diminished by modern health and safety requirements, is still beautiful. Neither shaped the rules of the future, although as we shall see from the Old Etonian Kennington Oval Cup ties against Darwen, the Field Game expressed somehow the deepest and most abiding flaws and glories of English football.

At Harrow football had always been played in the School Yard, where the goals did not face each other but were parallel, so that the ball had to be kicked around the end of a building. When it rained the boys played in the cloisters under the original Speech Rooms, and with a smaller ball. Throughout the nineteenth century, and perhaps earlier, they played passage football in their houses with a soft ball called a 'fug', which Charles Townsend Warner was to describe in 1895 as 'a squeaky creature made of hair, with a chamois leather skin'.

In 1803, as a consequence of building works, Harrow football moved to the playing fields. Although unofficial it was compulsory and controlled by the Monitors, and in the early 1820s was played on half-holiday afternoons with large numbers on each side. Boarding houses began to play each other at cricket in 1823, and the first recorded house football encounter was in October 1832, when the teams already had distinctive colours. Harrow claims to have invented that posh English slang whereby '-er' is added to the ends of words, and 'Footer' is one of its earliest coinings. Harrow still plays the game, and there is still no limit on the number of players, although eleven a side is usual, and they line up as three backs, four forwards and two wings on each flank. The object is to score 'bases' by kicking the ball through two uprights, and the oddity is the ball itself, which is made of three pieces of leather and shaped like a pork pie, about eighteen inches in diameter and twelve inches deep. It tends to soak up water and become extremely heavy, virtually impossible to head and painful if it strikes you. It may be a survival of something much older, because a sixteenth-century football found in Scotland in the 1990s had a similar construction.

The actual fields at Harrow were clay, which soon became a morass, and in the nineteenth century

Footer was never played in the rain. Much later, after the emergence of soccer, it was claimed that their experience of the awkward ball in muddy conditions was what made Old Harrovians such star dribblers. Footer was a hard-surface game that encouraged dribbling and allowed barging. But it forbade running with the ball in hand, and body-tackling, because in the yard or cloister they would have been dangerous. When Footer was transferred to a field it retained its dribbling and non-carrying culture, which is why it contributed to soccer. Carrying the ball and body-tackling were likewise banned from the Charterhouse cloister and the yards at Westminster, where football had also been played since the seventeenth century. By the 1840s, Westminster football was a game called Greens, and took place in Great Dean's Yard.

Greens is vividly described by Captain F. Markham of the Rifle Brigade, who published his memoirs in 1903 and had arrived at Westminster aged twelve in 1849. The goalposts were trees twenty yards apart at each end, and fifteen smaller boys known as 'Duffers' or 'Funk Sticks' were distributed as goalkeepers. The captains each picked a dozen or so of the best players, and more or less the rest of the school was shared out. This made about forty-odd a side, something like the Darwen game of 1820. A 'bully' was formed and contained the heavyweights. Was this a semi-upright linked scrum, like that which began the Eton Field Game, or opposed walls of men like Darwen versus Tottington? Markham does not say, but as at Darwen and Eton the ball was rolled in, and there was 'a general shinning match until it worked out'.

Lighter and faster boys who were 'dodging about outside' then tried to make progress towards the opposing goal, just as Ben Hart had hoped to do. But there were railings around the Yard, and the ball could be stuck against them for minutes on end, in a scrimmage that was called a 'rally'. Frederick Forshall, another Westminster memorialist, recalled the sheer misery of being crushed in a rally, and the anxiety of the small goalkeepers waiting in the cold.

Charterhouse called their 'rally' a 'squash', when in the seventy-yard-long cloister the ball could be stuck against a buttress for forty-five minutes, and jammed-in players were refreshed with lemons passed through the windows. Charterhouse arrived early at a line-up of a goalkeeper, a back and a variable number of forwards, but the buttresses were like the Westminster railings and the Eton wall: they made it impossible to progress beyond a folk football maul around the ball.

At the same time there was uncertainty everywhere over what sort of handling was permitted and what was not. Eton confined most of its mauling aspects to the Wall, and made the Field Game fluid: catching and body-tackling were banned, but the ball could be tapped down. In Darwen a goal had to be kicked in 1820, but in 1830 the ball could be carried over. Westminster allowed 'fist-punting', juggling the ball as one ran, until about 1852, and Harrow, Charterhouse and Westminster all allowed a catch and half-volley.

Of all the growing pains the most notable was at Rugby School, where in 1823 William Webb Ellis made a permissible catch but famously ran with the ball instead of kicking it. Today this is hailed as the origin of world rugby, but at the time it was controversial and was not fully incorporated into the school's rules until 1841. The reason for this is that what Webb Ellis did was not innovative but archaic: he had reverted to folk football. Since the only way to stop a man carrying the ball is to body-tackle him, people argued against it at the time, and it became the eventual reason for the split between soccer and rugby.

If we want to understand what football was like in 1830, or why in the 1870s men like Fergus Suter personified new tactics, it is easier to do so by watching not the soccer of today but rugby union. See, for example, the scrum half. Is he not the trundler-in of handloom weaver lore: except that the trundler-in does not seem to have played a further part in the game?

Some modern writers have implied that the hacking and violence of public school football and the Gentlemen Amateurs reveals a sadistic flaw in the ruling classes, but the Darwen versus Tottington working-class grudge match was at least as aggressive and even involved weaponry. The truth is that in team numbers, formations and attitudes rich and poor were similar: what was different about the way they played was offside. Did actual folk football have an offside law? Did the thirty- or thirteen-a-side Darwen games? Did offside spark the ill-feeling in the first Tottington encounter? The later accounts make no mention. Would the thirteen-a-side moorland game have developed offside if it had been able to continue? Impossible to know or even guess. What is clear is that football has swept the world because it is a simple game of amazing variety, and that the only illogical thing about it is the offside law. Yet every public school developed one, even Charterhouse in their cloister. It seems to have been their way to control the shapelessness of folk football, to set problems beyond mere violence, to give every player something to think about, and perhaps to meet schoolboy notions of fairness. And it forced people to take part, actually, and not loiter at a periphery. In the end the rules made a pastime a complex activity, with problems, standards and ethics of its own.

A significant moment in the history of the offside law, and indeed of football, occurred at Westminster. Years earlier, a rich former pupil had bequeathed to the school the ownership of St Vincent's Square in Pimlico. Throughout the 1840s there was politicking to take advantage of this and use the square as a playing field, and by about 1851 this was achieved. Over the next few years, Greens gave way to a new eleven-a-side game on St Vincent's Square called 'Fields'. Fields had narrow goals and a fixed goalkeeper. It kept the rules of Greens, and its three-man offside law, but with fewer men and no 'rallies' against the railings it was much more open. Captain Markham played both games but does not explain how or why Fields was the way it was. By the early 1850s Pimlico had begun to acquire the terraces we see today. It was a building site, and Markham's sharpest memory is that a hazard of playing on St Vincent's Square was that 'a gang of marble workers' would attempt to steal the football.

Fields was a clean break, a new game with dribbling but no body-tackling. Much the same happened at Charterhouse a decade later, when the boys realised what was happening at Westminster and decided to play outside the cloister as well as inside. Such were the steps that led to a general game called soccer, but that was not the conscious intention at the time. The first attempt to create a common game had been made in 1848, when Cambridge undergraduates from Eton and Shrewsbury School nailed compromise rules to a tree on Parker's Piece, but it did not attract wider interest. The fact was that low numbers of boys at school meant low numbers of school leavers. Too few old boys wanted to continue to play football as adults. The game could not yet be born.

The fall in numbers

Football's growth rate in the wider world is an incidental aspect of what makes the history of the public schools in the nineteenth century remarkable: the way in which they went from traditional success to odium and controversy, and back again to cultural triumph. As early as 1810 the *Edinburgh Review*, whose intellectual contributors knew about educational reforms in France and Prussia, raised objections to the English way.

What the schools taught, argued critics, was out of date. Aristocrats might arrive with private tutors but the curriculum was unsuited to modern life. It consisted of Greek and Latin by rote, haphazard religious instruction, but virtually nothing of science, languages or mathematics. Under the boarding house system buildings were old, sanitation was inadequate, and single beds and decent food cost extra. Above all, boys controlled other boys and had the power to flog them. The general culture, it was argued, was one of violence, bullying and homosexual scandals. Evangelical reformers like Dr Arnold at Rugby began to improve matters, but could do little about economic forces. After a slump in 1837 landed interests were pinched, and the 1840s were years of fluctuation. Fewer people spent money on sending their sons away, and *nouveau riche* industrialists like the Darwen mill owners were not yet convinced. The consequences were drastic.

In 1805 Harrow had some 350 pupils, a figure which then fell dramatically, as it did at similar institutions. By 1844 Harrow had only 69 pupils in three houses. Westminster, which had 300 in 1821, was down to 67 in 1841 and still only 96 by 1861. In 1835 Charterhouse had 100. In 1851 Uppingham had 28 boys and in 1854 Repton had 50. Meanwhile other schools were being founded: Cheltenham in 1840, Marlborough in 1843, Lancing in 1845. All these schools cost less than Harrow, and promised new ideas and a sounder moral tone. Only Eton maintained its size, which perhaps explains the scale of its football. At Harrow the fall in numbers is surely a reason for the reduction to an eleven-a-side house game; and at Westminster in the 1840s Greens must have involved almost every single pupil.

Football families

In 1801 the future Prime Minister, Sir Robert Peel, had been sent by his cotton millionaire father to Harrow (which he hated), but not many like him had followed. Just as a working lad like John Duxbury went into the mill aged seven, so the sons of merchants and manufacturers were placed in situations at fifteen or sixteen, after a few years at a local academy or grammar school. Too much education, it was felt, could unsettle a boy for commercial pursuits.

The eventual change in this attitude can be seen in the lives of the families who were to bring public school football to the Darwen area. There were four of them, the Walshes, the Kays, the Hornbys and the Ashtons, and of these the Ashtons owed their good fortune to their kinship with Darwen's dominant family, the Shorrocks. John Shorrock built one of the earliest mills and had two sons. Samuel went bankrupt but William, who married a daughter of the first mill builder, Thomas Eccles, was successful, ruthless and hated: in 1829 disaffected weavers tried to shoot him.

William's son, Eccles Shorrock, was as tough as his father but shrewder and more civilised, the first

Darwen master to wear a modern frock-coat. True to his Nonconformist heritage, he gave money towards the building of the Mechanics' Institute and the 1,400-seat Congregationalist Belgrave Chapel, he was a founder and committee man of the cricket club, and he believed in education so much that he hired a schoolteacher for his child employees in Bowling Green Mill long before the Government required him to do so. Eccles had a sister named Mary, who married Thomas Ashton, a loom manu-facturer from Clitheroe. Their son Eccles Shorrock Ashton arrived in 1827, and Ralph in 1829. After this birth Mary died, and the boys were adopted by their Uncle Eccles, who despite two advantageous marriages with local heiresses was childless. Thomas Ashton did marry again, and was to have a third son, William T. Ashton, whose life followed a traditional pattern: he was fifteen when in 1847 he arrived in Darwen to manage Brookside Mill. His son, James Christopher Ashton, was to be involved with the Walshes in the foundation of the football club, but William T. Ashton himself did not put money into the game, and neither did the Shorrocks. If they had, and if they had not been at the centre of the subse-quent political split in the town, the club might have been luckier.

The Walshes were lucky in that they survived the mixed fortunes of the 1840s. Nathaniel Walsh was born in 1814 on the family smallholding. There seems to have been some coal under the land, and Nathaniel used the capital this gave him to become a junior partner in the Darwen Paper Mills. Like the Shorrocks he was a Congregationalist, but in 1841 he married Ellen Altham in the Anglican parish church of Chipping, in rural north Lancashire. He is described in the register as a 'paper maker', and his father James as a farmer. Ellen's father is described as a yeoman, and the couple's paternal grandfathers were the witnesses. A year later the Paper Mills failed and Nathaniel lost his investment, but by 1844 he was in partnership with his brother, Ralph Walsh, in the Orchard Mill. They ran power looms and Ralph, who had no family of his own, kept the George inn, an old posting and commercial establishment. Nathaniel, having lost one career when the market collapsed, was lucky enough to be able to re-invest when it was still very low.

A similar instance of the way in which liquor businesses could accumulate cash and transform lives is provided by the Hindle family. The grandfather was a farmer who bought a pub called The Last Rose of Summer. His money enabled his grandsons to be sent to Blackburn Grammar School and become fully fledged members of the new mid-Victorian professional middle class. F. G. Hindle was a lawyer who became Darwen's Member of Parliament. His younger brother, Tom Hindle, became an accountant, and a stalwart of the football club as both player and secretary. Tom founded the Lancashire Football Association, and became a councillor of the Football Association itself; and to his dying day he denied that Love and Suter were professionals, although the entire world knew that they were.

Hindle was a common name in Darwen and Nancy

Hindle, an old lady interviewed with Duxbury and Chadwick in 1906, had in 1835 lived near the Town Field when it was built over. Her remark in her interview that the fortunes of the successful middle-class Hindles were founded on a pub, at a time when no self-respecting woman would enter one, as neither of my own cotton town grandmothers ever did, is a sidelight on local snobberies. Old Nancy and her print works engineer husband considered themselves every bit as good as the important Hindles. Hadn't she been born a Shorrock, great-niece of the original John Shorrock? It was just that her bit of the family failed, and came down in the world.

When young Nancy lived in a terraced cottage her distant cousin Eccles had a big house on the moors. He had seen sons of the Anglican Potter and Greenway wallpaper families go away to be educated, and true to his beliefs he sent his adopted son, Eccles Shorrock Ashton, to University College, London, at that time the only university in England open to Nonconformists. This more or less coincided with the decision of W. H. Hornby of Blackburn to send his eldest son, Edward, to Harrow School.

Hornby's family had been merchant grocers in Lancaster, and moved to Blackburn to invest their money in cotton. John Hornby was a putter-out who operated from a warehouse. His son William Henry was born in 1805 and in 1829 he built a water-driven twist mill at Brookhouse. He installed power looms in 1830, and in 1831 married the daughter of his father's erstwhile business partner. In 1841 Mrs Hornby had to flee from the back door of their mansion in King Street as unemployed rioters smashed in at the front, but William Henry brushed such inconveniences aside. His portraits show an active, shortish, peppery sort of person. He supported the Ten Hours Bill that regulated the working day, and allowed employees who devised improvements to machinery to profit from their ingenuity. He wanted what was best for them, but he wanted it for himself as well. By 1850 he had built four more mills, all driven by steam engines, plus houses for the workers and a walled sports ground.

The Hornbys had seven sons and four daughters, and five of the boys went to Harrow. Two of them played cricket for the school and the youngest, A. N. Hornby, became a legend of Lancashire and England cricket, and played a small but vivid role in the Darwen football saga. The Hornbys were Anglican and Tory and it was natural for them to use their wealth to be powerful and climb the conventional social ladder: to use Harrow to acquire the manner and mental furniture of gentlemen. They went on to buy landed estates and leisured lives.

That the outsider Walshes followed the fashion, and were accepted by Harrow, was an even surer sign of social change.

San Marco on the moors

In 1849 young Eccles Shorrock Ashton had returned from University College with his degree, and in 1851 he married Sarah Dimmock of the local paper-making family. Two years later his uncle died, aged forty-nine, and Eccles inherited everything: interests in cotton and paper mills, a sawmill and ten coal pits. He dropped the Ashton from his name and called himself Eccles Shorrock.

The years which followed were those in which Britain enjoyed the profits of its industrial dominance, and the likes of Eccles Shorrock, Jr and W. H. Hornby stood atop huge piles of them. Hornby acquired his estate in Cheshire and rode to hounds, and after Blackburn became a borough in 1851 was soon mayor and the town's Tory Member of Parliament. He operated a carve-up with his Liberal opponent and fellow mill owner Joseph Fielden, whereby neither allowed a second candidate on their ticket so that both were elected as the two with the most votes.

No such power games could be played in Darwen until 1854, when the town's elite took advantage of the 1848 Health Act. Parliament had decided that the social squalors of the new industrial towns should be tackled by local boards with the power to raise local rates, and Darwen's rich men won the right. At last they could wield local power, and spend local money, independently of Blackburn. Only property owners paid rates, and in local elections they were given from one to six votes according to the value of what they owned. This gave the elite a huge advantage and they voted themselves on to the board, and with Shorrock as Chairman awarded themselves its contracts for stone, coal, paper, uniforms and so forth, and embarked upon modernisation. In other words, they began to clear up the mess that their own activities had created. They installed piped water and a sewage system, paved the streets, and looked to impose upon the town their own ideals of self-help, cleanliness, hard work and education.

Eccles Shorrock was in his element. He was ambitious, serious, well-meaning, diffident and kind. He had a strong sense of what he owed the family, and of what they owed him in return, and, as can be the case with people of his advantages, he had a spoilt, stubborn streak that in the end ruined him, but at first spurred him on.

Was not everything around him prosperous? In 1850 female cotton operatives won the Saturday half-day off, and Nathaniel Walsh became the sole owner of Orchard Mill and added spinning machines. In 1853 Nathaniel built his mansion next door and called it Orchard Bank. In 1856 Shorrock himself built Hope Mill for his cousin William T. Ashton, and in 1859 he installed his first steam engine: as mills were enlarged to meet world demand water power could no longer drive them. The following year Nathaniel Walsh bought a more powerful steam engine, and Shorrock embarked upon his biggest project, the erection of India Mill. This was, and still is, an enormous structure with pointed Venetian gothic windows, and a chimney that was intended to represent the Campanile of San Marco. The chimney is 303 feet high, cost almost £14,000, and stands upon a single block of Darwen stone that required thirty-five horses to drag it into position.

The Football Association

Another consequence of the prosperity of the 1850s was that the public schools recovered their confidence and increased the number of their pupils. At Harrow this was to the credit of an inspirational headmaster named Charles Vaughan, who arrived in 1845. He had a charismatic personality that gave the impression of modernism and change, but did not perhaps alter very much about the way the school was, except to spend its increased income on building works. Vaughan was spoken of sometimes as a future Archbishop of Canterbury, but in 1859 he resigned without warning and his career fizzled out. Modern scholars incline to the view that he was bisexual, and forced out by his enemies, who threatened to expose his affair with a boy. But when Vaughan left, the school had more than 400 pupils, and this fact alone shows that in the world outside there would now be a critical mass of adults who wanted to play football.

Charles W. Alcock, who would become secretary of the Football Association, instigator of the FA Cup and the single most important person in early football history, also left Harrow in 1859. He was the son of a Sunderland ship-broker who had moved to Epping

Forest outside London, and when he left school he formed a football club called Forest with his brother, two other old Harrovians and some local friends. This was typical, after a sterile decade, of an invigorated appetite for the game. But the obstacle to expansion was the rules. There were so many different versions of football. What could or should be established in common?

Cambridge undergraduates had sought to answer this question since 1846, and posted their Parker's Piece rules in 1848. One of the 1840s Cambridge activists was J. C. Thring, who became a master at Uppingham School, and in 1862 he published rules for what he called 'The Simple Game'. Cambridge responded with the publication of its own rules, and the debate was public.

In September 1863, at the first of a series of five meetings that formed the Football Association, and agreed the Association Rules that gave the game its Harrow slang name 'soccer', twelve clubs were represented. Seven were from the London suburbs, one from the War Office, three from local London schools and only one from a great public school. This was Charterhouse, whose captain, Charles Cookson, attended to hear the discussion about the rules. It had been realised that to play outside the cloister there would have to be a different game, as Westminster Fields had been different.

Three weeks after the original meeting there was another, to which the major schools were sent invitations. Rugby, Eton and Winchester did not reply. Harrow and Westminster were cool. None attended.

'We cling to our present rules,' explained the Harrow captain, Charles Gordon Browne, 'and should be very sorry to alter them in any respect.'

There were three more meetings, in the course of which the clubs who favoured body-tackling left the discussions, and by December 1863 soccer was confirmed as an eleven-a-side, non-handling, non-body-tackling game with a rugby-style offside law: men had to be behind the ball when it was kicked. But without handling this rule made little sense and in 1866, the year in which Charles Alcock joined its committee, the Association changed to the three-man Westminster and Charterhouse offside law. This continued until 1925.

A talent for the game

Nathaniel Walsh's eldest son, James, arrived at Harrow School for the summer term of 1864. He was fourteen years old. Nathaniel himself, who as a teenager could have seen the Darwen thirteen-a-side football, was a founder committee member of Darwen Cricket Club, and presumably played, and both James and his youngest brother, George, had a gift for the game. James became a top batsman in the Harrow first eleven, and thus a member of the school's sporting aristocracy, the bloods who of a summer evening sauntered to other boarding houses to play yard cricket with a soft ball and a broomstick.

In the 1867 photograph of the team that played Eton at Lord's, James seems a slightish, sensitive person with a gentle expression: not unhappy or withdrawn, not arrogant or lordly like so many in the group photos of that epoch, not adopting the pose of a classical sculpture, but contained and private. This impression is reinforced by his later life in Darwen, when he accepted family and business responsibilities but would not take part in local politics; and as a fourteen-year-old new boy he must have been aware that he was entering a world in which many people were more privileged.

Even at home the Walshes were by no means the grandest. They employed 500 people when the Hornbys had 4,000 and the Shorrock interests some 3,500. By the 1871 Census their elder daughter, Mary, having married a local doctor and left home, Nathaniel and Ellen Walsh lived at Orchard Bank with their three sons, their younger daughter and three servants: a cook, a housemaid and a 'waitress'. W. H. Hornby had nine servants, including a coachman and a groom, and Shorrock's cousin W. S. Ashton employed a French governess.

One thing that it would be interesting to know about all these people is how they spoke. As Prime Minister, Sir Robert Peel always had a northern accent, and recordings of the aged William Gladstone convey echoes of one. Gladstone had been sent from his Liverpool merchant home to Eton in 1821. W. H. Hornby's accent was local, one presumes, but that of his son the great cricketer and footballer A. N. Hornby more 'proper'. Even high aristocrats dropped 'h' at the beginning and 'g' at the ends of words, supposedly because they spent so much of their childhoods with working-class nursery maids, so that it was the generation of the boys who went from Lancashire to Harrow, and came home with organised football, who were perhaps under the earliest pressure to conform to an educated, southern English 'Oxford' accent.

The speech of Darwen workpeople and footballers would have been very thick, with many dialect words as well as nicknames: 'Galloping Jack' for a local runner and 'Penny John's' for John Walmsley's Lodge Bank Mill. During the first Etonian Cup tie the

Darwen captain, James Knowles, known as 'Jem o' Bob's', was clattered by an opponent, who then apologised. Knowles replied, 'Apologies be hanged, after tha's welly killed a felly!' He is also said to have asked a player who made a wild kick, 'Wheer the hangment were tha puncin?'

That the Darwen elite sneered in private at such working-class ways is evident from the fact that James Christopher Ashton, son of William T. Ashton, wrote plays which he performed with other young people in the district's big houses. The one remembered was *Black Diamonds*, a comedy about a moment when coal prices were so high that even ordinary miners could afford to travel first class on the railway. Such theatricals, and charades, and home dances, and dinners of roast beef and boiled fowl in white sauce, may seem like nouveau riche scenes observed by Dickens, but the Ashtons did buy paintings, and with so many church choirs the town was soon to display a thriving amateur musical culture; and in the late 1860s there was a performance of *She Stoops to Conquer* in the Mechanics' Institute. There were balls in Blackburn, given by the likes of the officers of the local Volunteers. On the Fylde coast Blackpool had not quite taken off as a mass destination, but Southport already attracted people with money, and young men would parade its avenues in frilled shirts and tight trousers.

There is also an anomaly in the story of the Walshes and Darwen football, and it is that many anecdotal accounts say that Nathaniel had a fourth, older son, and one speculates that this may have been

W. T. Walsh, who was an early captain of the football club, secretary for a time, an umpire in the first Old Etonian tie, and the writer of provocative letters to the *Darwen News*. Other evidence points to W. T. Walsh having less money than the Orchard Bank family, and there is no local birth register of a W. T. Walsh of more or less the right age to fit the events, and none mentioned in the town directories. This is not altogether surprising. There are very few mentions of any of the Darwen players, because they were not ratepayers: they were working-class men who rented, or lived with their mothers, who are not mentioned either. Again, so many Darwen people had the same names that it can be impossible even in a Census to know who was who. It is one of the fascinations of the Oval Cup ties: in the one team important, written-up and recorded men, and in the other the unrecorded and more or less unknowable, who nobody realised were historic until it was too late. Of the two professionals, Fergus Suter is among the big-wigs in the *Dictionary of National Biography*, but Jimmy Love is faceless and lost, save for the vital goals he scored.

What is evident is that the Orchard Bank Walshes had a talent for ball games, and one tends to link W. T. Walsh with them for that reason alone. Perhaps he was a cousin in lesser circumstances. Whoever he was, he cannot have been the only person to feel intense local pride when a man who had been born on a smallholding at the edge of Dirty Darren saw his son open the Harrow batting at Lord's.

Find Fags

James Walsh would have sat an entrance exam to be accepted by Harrow, and finding a house was about influence, who you knew and what you could afford. Housemasters owned their school houses, which meant that academically minded men could make more money as masters at Harrow than in many other places, and this attracted a fruitful variety of personalities: deep humanists, eccentrics, dreamers, careerists. James Walsh's housemaster, E. H. Bradby, tended to the latter. He was remembered as a boring teacher, had been educated at Rugby (a fashionable reformist credential) and rented his house before buying it in 1863. He then renovated and extended, so that when James arrived work was in progress, to make the place pleasing to interested parents, to attract more of them and as an investment: in 1867 Bradby left to pursue his star as headmaster of Haileybury, but kept his ownership of the Harrrow house and leased it to the former Cambridge mathematician 'Vanity' Watson.

Altogether, Bradby must have seemed to someone like Nathaniel Walsh to be a good choice, an educated version of the sort of entrepreneurial mindset he understood. James, however, had to start at the bottom of the heap, as a Find Fag at the beck and call of sixth formers. Harrow's structure was contradictory in that boys could not enjoy sixth form privileges or become a Monitor until they were sixteen. Yet they ascended the school hierarchy by their academic results, so that older dullards could be flogged for bad work, while clever younger boys were sixth formers without privileges. Top sports people were a favoured breed, as the verse tells us:

> Jerry's a monitor bold
> Champion at rackets and fives
> Cricketers youthful and old
> Worship his cuts and his drives.

James Walsh had the luck to become such a person, but at first he would have been harried here and there. Nor could he have had much contact with an older acquaintance like A. N. Hornby: only after three years could boys bring friends from other houses into their own, so that generally speaking wider associations began in the sixth form, and the house experience was intense.

Even today Harrow on its Hill feels cut off from the rest of the world, and in the 1860s that feeling must have been overwhelming, not least because fags sent to fetch a sixth former's breakfast from the High Street shops (bacon and eggs in greaseproof paper) had to dodge the scaffolding, mortar dust, spoil heaps and upheavals of building works: Victorian gothic wonders were being erected and boarding houses jazzed up. The entire school was being changed and enlarged, and not just physically.

A fag who dodged along the street with someone's breakfast had already done one and a half hours of school, and Second Schools ran from ten to one thirty. There was another three quarters of an hour in the afternoon. From a Find Fag, James would have progressed to what was called a Boy, and done odd day jobs such as lighting fires and running errands. The duties depended on the ratio of sixth formers to fags. Boys could be exempted for a week, or put on again next day if they were unsatisfactory. In summer school ended at six, and was followed by tea, cricket until eight thirty, and then lock-up. At the end of that first summer term James must surely have acquired a little reflected glory from the fact that he was acquainted with the seventeen-year-old A. N. Hornby, who was about to make his cricket debut against Eton at Lord's.

Even then Hornby was a star. He was the 'Little Wonder' at five foot three and less than six stone, 'bat and all'. He was nicknamed 'Monkey' for his agility, ferocity and cheekily simian jawline. In the team photo for that year he is perched on the shoulders of his captain, C. F. Butler, like a mascot or a child among the grown-ups. Over the two days of that match in 1864 16,000 people attended, and the first day's receipts were £570. There was no comparable football crowd until the 1880s. Club football games around London in 1864 would be watched by a few dozen friends and idlers.

It would probably have been in the first term of 1865 that James Walsh became a Night Fag. They were the elite of the lower world and entrusted with at least one very delicate task. At that time many books were sold with the pages bound but uncut, and a Night Fag would slit open his sixth former's volumes. He would also answer calls after lock-up, and let down the wall beds that were a Harrow speciality. A prankster could set up a bed so that it collapsed when sat upon, and it was possible to shut a boy up in one. Some boys even slept in a chair, which was called a Frowster. Tollying up – lighting a candle after dark – was a sixth form privilege.

When A. N. Hornby and James Walsh went home in 1865 they found Lancashire in distress. The American Civil War was raging, and the Northern blockade of Confederate ports restricted the export of raw cotton. What ensued was the so-called Cotton Famine. Most of the mills in Lancashire were closed. In Darwen 10,000 people were put out of work and the construction of India Mill was suspended.

Eccles Shorrock was foremost among the Darwen masters who treated their laid-off operatives with generosity, and at a famous meeting in Manchester's Free Trade Hall out-of-work people sent Abraham Lincoln a message of support in his fight against slavery. Then the war ended, supplies were again reliable, and there was an even more spectacular boom. But the episode reverberated. My grandfather was born during the Cotton Famine, like the child in Samuel Laycock's great dialect poem 'Bonny Brid', and often told me how the Famine had seemed to workpeople of his parents' generation: an omen, somehow, almost biblical, its meaning never fully clear.

The Famine did not, of course, affect the 1865 Eton and Harrow match.

How could it? By now this was more than a cricket fixture. It was an event in the London season, when Parliament was in recess and the gentry and the well-to-do from all over the country gathered in London for three months of balls, parties and attendance at sporting events. Then in August they went away to shoot game birds. At Lord's the first day's crowd was huge because that was the day on which people went to be seen. There would be some 400 carriages, taken to the ground and unhitched the day before. Ladies wore new dresses and deployed parasols, acquaintances were renewed, courtships continued and picnics served from hampers and ice-boxes. Working-class supporters wore fancy costumes, got drunk around the Tavern and started fights.

At this time the batting crease was not a whitewashed line but a groove, brushed out before each session of play, and there were no boundary ropes. Hits were run out. It was in the 1865 match that A. N. Hornby chased a ball among the carriages and knocked an old gentleman over. Hornby was described as 'even then a terror running short runs'.

The Clarendon Commission

One subject of conversation among the 1865 crowd at Lord's was, we may be sure, the Clarendon Commission of Enquiry into the Public Schools. This had been set up in 1861 and reported in 1864, and its recommendations were hotly discussed until the Government did something about them in 1866. Educational reformers had found it easy to criticise English schools, but hard to convince politicians and taxpayers that there should be a continental-style national system funded by central government. On the one hand there was a hotch-potch of vested interests and ancient institutions to consider, but on the other the debate would not go away. When in 1861 the Census showed that 27 per cent of males and 39 per cent of females were illiterate, the public schools must have seemed to practical politicians and the Treasury to be the least of their worries: but they had to address them, if only to appear morally right thinking, and they did so in classic Establishment fashion by setting up a Commission of Enquiry chaired by Lord Clarendon.

In theory Clarendon could have recommended radical changes or even closure. In practice most members of the Commission had been educated at the establishments they were investigating, and the legislation which followed let the schools carry on with a veneer of reforms. This ensured that hence-forth English education would be class-based. There would be no national system as there was in France or Prussia. Rich people would buy one sort of educa-tion, grammar schools would provide a percentage of scholarships for the clever, local religious denomin-ational schools would continue, and the Government would do the rest. A public school, as the Old Harrovian F. M. Norman was to write in 1899, became 'not so much a place where book learning is to be acquired, as a sphere for the formation and developments of the habits, character and physique of an English gentleman'.

What Parliament had sanctioned was a compromise, a political and financial easy option, and it was almost by default that the public schools created administra-tors with the wherewithal to run an empire: the system of boys governing boys gave people experi-ence of the use and abuses of power from a very early age. The moral code which would inspire and bind these men together was neither prescribed nor predicted, but it sprang to life nevertheless, and almost of its own accord. Its intellectual reference points were heroic moments in English history, and its ideal of behaviour came from something that the boys had always loved and done for themselves. In other words, they were to find themselves indoctrinated through sport.

The great cricket field of life

Vaughan's successor as headmaster of Harrow was Montague Butler. He was only twenty-six, and soon grew a beard to seem older. He was a disingenuous enthusiast, a sort of perpetual schoolboy-cum-scholar himself, and at the same time a relentless fundraiser, networker and inventor of traditions that he passed off as ancient. Early in Butler's career a master named Robert Quick resigned because he objected to the prevalence of games at Harrow, to the importance attached to them by the boys, and to the staff's lack of control. Harrow games, he said, were 'a world in which the schoolmaster has as much share as the coastguard officer in the life of the smuggler'.

Within a short time this situation changed. Masters became not only drug barons, as it were, but condom-swallowing mules as well. Butler's assistant master, E. E. Bowen, was an avid Footer player and codified its rules. Another Harrow teacher, Dean Farrar, coined the phrase 'the great cricket field of life'. It was a decisive moment in the history of the British mindset, and it is all the more interesting when we remember that at Rugby in the 1820s Dr Arnold had encouraged football not to mould the boys, but to keep them on the school premises and out of the countryside, and that between 1827 and 1832 Samuel Butler, the headmaster of Shrewsbury, had actually banned the game.

The masters and the system had invented neither cricket nor football, but now they took control and made use of them.

Songs

James Walsh was joined at Bradby's by his middle brother, Charles, in the summer of 1867, the very moment at which masters took control of games. Since 1852 Harrow sport had been co-ordinated by the Philathletic Club, which met in rooms over the school bookshop, and masters now joined the discussions. In particular, E. E. Bowen gave Footer a more organised fixture calendar and wrote down its rules: he seems to have been most determined to maintain the Footer tradition, and to protect it against soccer. Also in 1867 there was a transformation in Songs, that unique expression of the Harrow self-romance.

Boys had started a Musical Society in 1857, the year incidentally in which Fergus Suter was born in a Glasgow tenement, and in 1862 the Society engaged John Farmer to conduct choral music. Farmer was the son of a Nottingham lacemaker sent on business to Zurich, where he married a Swiss woman and met the exiled composer Richard Wagner, whom he assisted on a production of *Lohengrin*. Farmer was never employed by the school as such. He seems to have been recommended to the Society, which like sport had money from school bills, by the housemaster

B. F. Westcott. *The Harrow Almanack* for 1866 let slip the inspiration for the scheme when it said that Farmer adapted the tunes of German student songs but gave them 'a distinctive colouring of his own'.

Beginning with Westcott's, Farmer and his harmonium would visit houses and conduct singing parties about once a fortnight. He became famous for idiosyncratic turns of phrase. A boy who could not sing sounded like 'a bogey in a water-butt' or 'a weasel in a band-box'. A butterfly collector, and there must have been many butterflies on those leafy slopes, was 'a beetle Joseph'. At first Farmer met hostility, the Grove boys greeting an early visit with a shower of dirty boots, and the first songs had Latin words. But when Walsh's housemaster, the ever-pragmatic Bradby, wrote English lyrics the thing took off.

The power of Songs to strengthen a school over and above a house tradition was soon grasped, and in 1867 E. E. Bowen wrote the words to the cricket song 'Willow the King'. Five years later he was to write 'Forty Years On', which became the School Song, thundered out at Whole School Songs, Founder's Days and Reunion Dinners. It is of course about football, as are many others in the repertoire.

> They tell us the world is a scrimmage
> And life is a difficult run . . .

was a verse written much later, in 1885, by a master named E. W. Hawson. It is a classic expression of sport as the way to know life.

Willow the King

Harrow cricket was a production line and between 1848 and 1868 they lost only twice to Eton. The groundsman, Gilby, was a professional who bowled at the boys, and there was a formal practice system whereby each boy batted until he had scored ten no matter how many times he was out. Another peculiarity was that there were three weeks of cricket in the autumn term, before Footer restarted. This enabled players new to the sixth form game to get a start, and the school captain to have a good look at them, before serious business resumed the following year.

James Walsh was brought along by this method. He was picked for Bradby's when he was fifteen and the next year played house Footer as well. In September 1866 he made his cricket debut for the school, batting in the middle order, and in May 1867 he was promoted to be the regular opener, with W. Renn as his partner, and enjoyed a run of good form.

There can be no doubt that in the 1860s cricket pitches and outfields were poor, bumpy and erratically mown, and that this accounts for the low scores in most matches, and for the use of a field placing like long stop. The Eton captain, Neville Lyttelton, wrote in his comments about the 1863 match: 'Our long stop was very good at Eton, but the pace of Lord's beat him.' Older histories say that as pitches improved and boys arrived from preparatory schools with their technique already formed, the 'Harrow style' of batting died out. Watch the ball, open your shoulders, and hit. Would we call this slogging? Very likely, but it was probably still pretty much the way in 1867.

The 1867 Eton match itself is historic because it saw the first use in cricket of boundary ropes, partly as a consequence of Hornby's collision in 1865 and partly because of a scandal in 1866. What happened in the 1866 match was as follows. The Eton captain, Lubbock, and his partner, Farmer, were batting when a ball was hit into the crowd and thrown back by a spectator. The batsmen assumed that the ball was dead, but a fielder threw down Farmer's wicket and he was given run out. This led to an uproar in which Lubbock's temper blew. Anger spread to the crowd and there were nasty incidents. The Princess of Wales left the ground in dismay and play was suspended. Lubbock refused to back down. Next morning the dispute was resolved by Farmer, who declined an offer to bat on.

This fracas was discussed in sporting circles for a long time, and would have been remembered by James Walsh and his brothers, and recounted to the Darwen footballers, when twelve years later Lubbock played against them for Old Etonians. On 12 July 1867 Eton had seven of their previous year's eleven (although not Lubbock) and were expected to win.

They batted first and made 208. Harrow made 173, Walsh being caught and bowled for 13. The Eton second innings, in which Walsh took a catch, made 221, and Harrow were set a target of 257 to win. These were two-day matches and in the time available Harrow reached 78 for one. Walsh was 28 not out. 'The fielding didn't quite come off,' wrote W. B. Money, Harrow captain at both cricket and Footer, but in the second innings 'Harrow pluckily played an uphill game.' They had done well to draw, we might think. On the fashionable first day there had been 12,000 spectators.

In all games – sixth form, house and for the school – James Walsh scored in 1867 510 runs at an average of 16.4, and was the second highest scorer behind Money himself. In school matches he was top scorer, with 264 at an average of 20.4, good figures on the pitches of those days, and he was awarded the Ebrington Challenge Cup for Batting. Then he left school and went home, to manage Orchard Mill.

Art treasures

Anecdotally, all three Walsh brothers attended Harrow, but there is no record at the school of George having done so. This is not necessarily conclusive, since more than one well-known Harrovian – for example, the early photographer Henry Fox Talbot – left little or no mark in the records. But Charles Walsh is in the cricket scorebooks for April 1868 and George, in the 1870s a high-scoring batsman for Darwen, is nowhere to be found.

At the end of that summer term Charles left Harrow and went home to excitement, prosperity and the event that was the high noon of the mill-owning elite, and the most spectacular demonstration of their paternalistic idealism. India Mill was finished, but before the machinery was installed Eccles Shorrock filled it with his Art Treasures Exhibition.

This displayed 486 oils, 423 watercolours, scenic photographs of Egypt, Yorkshire and the Lake District, and models of engines, pumps, incubators, light-houses, ships and mechanical tools. There were arrangements of potted palms, drill by the Rifle Volunteers, Strauss waltzes, local choirs and a display by a troupe of Manchester gymnasts entitled 'Assault at Arms'. The guest of honour on opening day was

Lord Hartington, who must have been much gawped at by respectable chapel-goers because he was known as a libertine whose mistress was a famous courtesan nicknamed 'Skittles'. He was also a Liberal Party grandee, a sometime Cabinet minister, and heir to the Duke of Devonshire.

There were thirteen pictures from the Duke's Chatsworth, including Canalettos, Gainsboroughs and Claude Lorrains, and others by Dürer, Teniers, Turner, David Cox, Tissot, Frith and Whistler. One of the Whistlers was an up-to-the-minute Impressionist seascape that was poorly reviewed. Shorrock lent four pictures and his Ashton relatives twelve. Many works were bought for resale and the exhibition made a profit of over a thousand pounds, which was given to the building of a Congregationalist school. One item of expenditure was £7 14*s*. 11*d*. for the hire of a 'Piping Bullfinch'. Whether this was a mechanical toy or an actual bird is not stated. But for a while great masterpieces did hang in a cotton mill.

Unfortunately, as seems to be the way with high noons, 1868 was the year in which the Darwen elite began to divide politically.

Antidisestablishmentarianism

William Gladstone the Liberal and Benjamin Disraeli the Conservative were the heroic opponents of mid-Victorian politics, the Frazier and Ali of House of Commons debates, the representatives of not just party politics, but of two different ways of apprehending life, and of how to respond to it. As a young man Gladstone was obsessed like many evangelicals of the day by the importance of saving souls, and the idea that politics might be conducted on religious principles, and to this end he espoused moral causes: all too often, said his critics, he found a new one when he needed to sidestep his opponents.

Disraeli was the Jewish outsider who had used his talents as a novelist to get on. Ambiguous, distrusted, financially insecure until late middle age, he called England two nations, rich and industrial poor, and perhaps it was because he was not quite English himself that he had a prophetic sense of what the country actually felt, but had not yet admitted to itself. Gladstone, perhaps, thundered always about what the country *should* feel.

Ostensibly the Conservatives were the party of privilege and stability, and the Liberals of careful reform, but in 1867 it was Disraeli who did the sidestepping. Lord Derby was the Tory Prime Minister in the Lords and Disraeli led the party in the Commons. He had always admired an earlier election manoeuvre whereby, as he said, Sir Robert Peel 'caught the Whigs bathing and stole their clothes', and in the 1867 election he persuaded Derby to do the same. They stole Gladstone's policies, and promised to give millions of working men the vote, and to pass social legislation, and were duly returned to power.

They did not keep it for long. In the autumn of 1868 their diehard backbenchers rebelled and forced another election. Gladstone won, but he had to endorse Disraeli's measures, and come up with some new ones of his own.

Politics mattered in mid-Victorian England because over the last decades they had improved people's lives, and they mattered at a local level because there were no mass media and everything had to be discussed locally. In 1868 Darwen was still part of the Blackburn constituency, and there was a scandal.

John Gerald Potter of the wallpaper family was a university-educated man who had long objected to the carve-up between the Tory member W. H. Hornby and the Liberal Joseph Fielden, whereby each allowed the other to take one of the two seats. For one thing it meant that Darwen itself had no direct representation. In 1865 Potter had put himself up as a second Liberal candidate. He failed but stood again in 1868. There were numerous new electors and both Hornby and Fielden sent circulars to their mill overlookers, telling them to instruct people how to vote. This was illegal, and after a parliamentary enquiry Hornby and Fielden were unseated. In response they each put up one of their sons as replacements, and Potter and Darwen were foiled again.

When Parliament sat, it soon became clear what Gladstone's new moral policy would be: an attempt, in the face of increasingly violent nationalism, to solve the Irish problem.

We may see with hindsight that on the question of British policy in Ireland Mr Gladstone's instinct to offer Home Rule, and to separate the Anglican Church there from the State, was correct. At the time many disagreed with him on grounds of material interest or political ideology, and some because they believed that a State Church was the one guarantee that society cared for its people; one such believer, and a man much involved in social duties, was the Reverend Philip Graham of Darwen.

Graham was born in Kirklinton in Cumberland in 1822, and became a curate in Darwen in 1852. His politics were Liberal, he taught at the Mechanics' Institute, was preferred to Manchester, and in 1855 returned to Darwen, when he married Jane, the young second wife and now widow of Eccles Shorrock, Sr. She was the heiress of John Bradwood of Turncroft, and brought with her seven coal mines, quarries, farms and a handsome mansion. Graham was said to have 'jumped out of the pulpit and into the coal pit'. He resigned his curacy and managed his wife's business interests with great success.

In 1864 they built St John's Church with £11,000

of their own money and in 1866 added a school. Jane died in 1867. A year later Graham was so incensed by Mr Gladstone that he called a meeting in the school and formed a local branch of the Conservative Party. His aides were a mill manager, a mechanic and newsagent, a plasterer and the Reverend Charles Greenway, rentier inheritor of the Greenways who had arrived to mill paper in the 1790s. His supporters were working men and, as time passed, individuals from most of the principal families.

Antidisestablishmentarianism is a long and comical word to describe a forgotten political stance, but it tells us something else as well.

Philip Graham regarded Gladstone as a careerist who had betrayed his own ideals, but Disraeli knew better. He knew that behind the speechifying what had changed was society. It had gelled into layer upon layer of a class system in which most people felt secure, even when they wanted to improve things. Even creations of working-class self-defence like the Co-operative Societies had become part of the capitalist fabric.

Darwen Co-operative Society was founded in 1860 to provide 125 members with cheap food. By the late 1870s it had 3,000 members out of the town's 30,000 population, had built a huge public hall at a cost of £11,000, and had the power to create new businesses. One of its butchery suppliers, Ralph Ashton, had begun as a throstle spinner in the New Mill, and Robert Preston used his grocery profits to rework old coal pits. In earlier decades articulate and impassioned ordinary people had been machine-smashers, readers of illegal radical newspapers, and organisers of torchlit meetings on the moors. In the late 1860s such resistance was peaceful: trade unionism bent on better deals and, for the lower middle class, activism in the Darwen Ratepayers' Association.

The liberal mill owners who dominated the Health Board did not hesitate to spend freely, and in 1871 they made a typical decision. Parliament allowed local authorities to add a penny to every pound of rates they raised and spend it on a Free Library. The elite took advantage. The Mechanics' Institute became the Free Library, which meant that its funding had been secured, but transferred from private purses to the public. Darwen was the only non-borough in England to take this opportunity, which is ample proof of its individuality, and the Library flourishes to this day, its Local History Collections on which so much of this book has depended proudly maintained in what were the Institute's back rooms. None of which stopped the shopkeepers and small businesses who contested Board elections for the Ratepayers' Association from protesting that the Liberal elite overspent, and in 1872 the Ratepayers won control.

At this a piqued Eccles Shorrock, Jr resigned because, as he put it, 'there is no freedom of action'. In other words, if he could not control affairs just as he pleased, he would not be involved in them at all. This was ironic, because the new Board's failure to maintain investment was in 1874 to be blamed for the pollution of the town water supply, and a cholera epidemic. The Liberals regained power but with a new front man in William Snape. The lustre of Eccles Shorrock had begun to tarnish.

Turton Football Club

National politics were reported at length in the Blackburn papers, and cricket scores given in detail, but there was no mention of what was the beginning of modern football. Why would there be? It was an odd little event, organised by a teenager, when in December 1871 John Charles Kay left Harrow and persuaded W. T. Dixon, the headmaster of Chapeltown village school, to call a meeting and start Turton Football Club. John's father, James, had agreed to be president, John himself was elected secretary, and forty-eight locals from the hamlets of Chapeltown, Edgworth, Entwistle and Qualtor paid a shilling each to join. It was a fair sum for a local mill or farm boy. How much the moorland village blokes knew about public school football or the foundation of the FA it is impossible to say, but they were enthusiastic when offered the chance to join an organised club, and there were enough of them for Turton to play scratch games among the members.

Chapeltown was where Darwen had played Tottington in 1830, and the Kays had bought Turton Tower, a Jacobean house a few hundred yards away. They were the rentier descendants of John Kay, the Preston-born farm boy who was a mechanical genius and in 1733 had invented the 'flying shuttle', which enabled handloom weavers to do the same amount of piece-work in a third of the time. Typically, most of them seem to have opted for more leisure and, presumably, football.

John Charles Kay himself was one of those people who are more enthusiastic about games than good at them. He arrived at Harrow in the term at the end of which Charles Walsh left. They were in different houses but knew each other at home. Kay did not make the house Footer eleven but he was in its cricket team, and won its internal quarter-mile race. He was to leave Turton after his marriage in 1877, so that although he had a lifelong involvement in cricket administration, his contribution to soccer was as brief as it was vital. Almost as soon as Kay had founded Turton he realised, like Gentleman Amateur club secretaries around London, that games among the members were not enough. What was needed were outside opponents.

Early in 1872 his fellow Old Harrovians the Walsh brothers rose to his promptings with the formation of Darwen Football Club.

Watch-house

That there had been for some time football matches between teams drawn from the workers in various mills and foundries in Darwen and Blackburn is impossible to prove but very likely. The Hornbys had their factory sports ground and W. H. Hornby is said to have been benign when mill windows were smashed by errant balls. In the later 1870s there were numerous reports of factory games, and the meeting which began the Darwen club was called after a match between teams representing the Walshes' Orchard Mill and William. T. Ashton's New Mill in Union Street.

Ashton's 23-year-old son James Christopher, the erstwhile dramatist, was his managing partner in this mill, and with the Walsh brothers attended the meeting. It took place in the watch-house of Orchard Mill. Watch-houses were separate buildings at the gates of a mill, or sometimes part of the office block, where the nightwatchmen based themselves. They were also, in the sterner discipline of those days, holding spaces. People who came late for work would have to wait in the watch-house to know whether they would be let in to work or sent home and lose a day's pay.

There would as well be other people, mostly women, who wanted casual or occasional work. They would sit in the watch-house in the hope that they would be called to take the place of absentees, sick people or ones sent away. My grandfather, when before 1914 he was manager of the Oldham Velvet Company, would stand at the gate, order it closed at seven thirty, and if necessary pick some hopefuls from the watch-house.

Some of this activity would be due to families and neighbours standing in for each other with the connivance of spinners and overlookers, and turning people away seems to have ended with the labour shortage of the First World War. Even so, when I worked in a mill in the 1950s, there were nearly always children and neighbours bringing sick notes and explanations, and people being sent messages and asked if they could come in. A mill was a world. It drew on its surrounding streets and had simple tasks even for disabled people. Today they would be at home on benefits, but for a century and a half they had a respected place in that dust-heavy, steam-heated, machine-screeching, oil-smelling civilisation.

A watch-house would have a table, a bench or two, the mill's keys on a board or in a glass case, the watchmens' paraphernalia and probably the mill fire brigade's gear. It was a convenient and obvious place for a meeting, although one in which some workpeople had at one time or another felt uneasy.

Fifty years later three men who had played in the 1872 mill game and attended the meeting, Peter Duckworth and Eli Kirkham of Orchard Mill and

Moses Neville of New Mill, were interviewed and said that Darwen's first match was against the Hornbys' Brookhouse Mills team. A. N. Hornby played for Brookhouse, who won 3–1 on a rented field in Darwen.

Gave him pause

We see again and again, and at all social levels, that to find opponents and agree rules with them was the problem of early football, and Turton essayed a mixture of Harrow and Association rules. They allowed the flip-up catch and the three yards in which to half-volley, and the playing area was long, like those at Harrow, and the goals twelve feet wide. They are supposed to have marked them out with lamp-standards borrowed from Turton railway station. Their first recorded fixtures were in 1872, against Blackburn and Darwen. Since there was no Blackburn club at this time we may assume that this was the Brookhouse Mills team. A. N. Hornby certainly played for the Blackburn side, and his 'rash, truculent, warm-hearted' character caused great controversy in a game that was characterised by much brutality and saw two Turton players carried off.

Hornby then turned out for Darwen against Turton, and this time young Robert Kay, aged fourteen and on school holidays from Harrow, was detailed to mark him. Robert was a big lad who played for his house, and it was said that when he tackled Hornby 'he gave him pause'. Not that Hornby was ever repressed for long. He was already Lancashire's cricket captain, a dashing front-foot batsman and a fine cover point: his legacy to the county, interesting in the light of comments on Eton and Harrow games, was his insistence upon fielding discipline and practice.

Some time in the summer of 1872 Francis Thompson, a thirteen-year-old chemist's son from Preston, was taken to Old Trafford to see his Lancashire heroes play Gloucestershire; decades later, near the end of his unhappy life, they played on in his poetry.

As the run-stealers flicker to and fro, to and fro –
O my Hornby and my Barlow long ago!

The aggressive, reckless, rich and selfish amateur Hornby, and the stone-walling working-class professional Dick Barlow: a classic combination who deserve their couplet, which is so simple in its rhyme and so elegiac in its dying fall. Barlow once carried his bat for five through a Lancashire innings that lasted two and a half hours, and in the 1870s the joke was the number of times that Hornby's attempted singles ran him out.

Barley Bank

In March 1872 Nathaniel Walsh collapsed and died aged fifty-eight while on a visit to the Fylde coast. Henceforth Orchard Mill was run by the Exors of N. Walsh. James Walsh had more responsibilities, and in the late 1870s he played less cricket than one might have expected. He had previously turned out for the football team with his brothers George and Charles and W. T. Walsh (if he was a brother), as well as Hubert Ashton, the younger son of W. S. Ashton and nephew of Eccles Shorrock, Jr, the calico printer Joshua Baron, and a member of the Place family, who owned a brick and tile works. In Darwen terms this was a team of gentlemen and it was no doubt these people who instigated the move in 1873 whereby the football club amalgamated with the cricket and shared the Barley Bank ground. Barley Bank was in the middle of town, overlooked by Orchard Mill, and had a pavilion and a bad slope; but it was a walled enclosure, albeit with gaps instead of turnstiles, which meant that it could accommodate a crowd and take gate money in a modern, spectator sport sense. As a result, when success came, the football club was set up to take advantage.

By the time of the move, even though local union

agreements differed from town to town, and sometimes even mill to mill, men as well as women workers in the Lancashire cotton trade had won Saturday half-days off. This released them to be both players and spectators, with momentous consequences, although it would be a year or two before their presence was felt. Middle-class men were already involved. Thomas Duxbury, grandson of weavers but educated at night school and manager of the new gas and water works, was chairman of Darwen Football Club, the young accountant Tom Hindle player-secretary, and George Walsh, the cashier of Orchard Mill, was treasurer.

The vice-president was Charles Costeker, who was twenty-two when he arrived from London in 1871, and as his obituary put it seventy years later 'he was as vigorous and active intellectually as his physique was commanding and elevated'. Photographs show an amused hawk face and a long stride. He arrived with cash to buy into a law practice and was soon clerk to both the Board of Health and county magistrates. Costeker made his fortune in Darwen and bestrode its little world like a colossus. He was a Conservative but a born conciliator and operator, a new man for the new times that came after 1874, when the working men whom Disraeli had enfranchised swept him into power and made the Lancashire cotton towns Conservative for the next thirty years.

When the Darwen FC Committee looked around for fixtures, they soon realised that it was easier to arrange them with clubs that had grounds a short walk from the railway line, and this is the pattern that emerged. By 1874 there were teams in Bolton, Eagley (five minutes from the station at Bromley Cross), Turton, Darwen, Blackburn and Church.

As opportunities increased, however, so did opposition to John Kay's Harrow-based Turton rules, and indeed to any kind of handling. Harrow rules meant nothing to working men and the start of the Football Association Cup in 1872 had caught the imagination. People argued that it was the Harrow rule about catching, and challenges to the catcher, that led to the serious injuries which could leave men unable to work. In modern rugby a catcher cannot be hit if he does not have the ball in his hands, but in the 1870s a man could be hit before he received the ball, and before his balance and his eye-line were adjusted to withstand the assault. No wonder injuries ensued, or that one of them befell George Walsh himself, so that after 1875 he did not play football again.

Turton, and presumably Darwen, seem also to have played sometimes with a Harrow-shaped ball, another thing which cannot have suited the locals, who had played informal street and pub football with a round ball.

John Kay saw the logic of these reservations and at its 1874 annual general meeting Turton voted to adopt Association Rules. A. N. Hornby disagreed, and stomped off to play rugby for Preston Grasshoppers and England, although as late as 1880 he played soccer sometimes for Blackburn Rovers. By then he had married Ada Ingram, whose father founded the *London Illustrated News*. Darwen tried to play on with Harrow rules, but the injury to

George Walsh and Turton's refusal to meet them except under FA rules were decisive, and by the end of 1875 they were an Association club with a team of mostly working-class players.

The first Partick friendly

W. Kirkham, an overlooker, was one of the first cotton operatives to join the soccer-playing club. He was a very skilful forward and a resourceful person, and by the 1881 Census was twenty-six years old and living with his wife, Lucy, and their two-year-old daughter, Nellie, in Tower Street, Darwen, facing the Paper Company's works and a short walk from several mills, including the India and William T. Ashton's Hope. Because Nellie's age fits the dates, she was surely the babe in arms taken in 1879 to the Remnants Cup tie.

Kirkham is an important link in soccer history because he left Darwen to take a job in Glasgow. It is not known why or precisely when, but it was probably in the middle of 1875. When he was settled in Glasgow he joined Partick, the local district's football club, and wrote to the Darwen secretary, Tom Hindle, to say that he could arrange a visit for a friendly.

By this time there were international matches between England and Scotland and a few friendly encounters with the leading London sides. It is improbable that anyone from Darwen had seen these games, but they would have read about them in the new *Athletic News* and in the *Football Annual* edited by Charles Alcock. They would know that the Scots played a different and much-discussed brand of football to the English, and now here was Kirkham as a regular participant in it. They would have been both curious and excited, and the subsequent friendly match seems to have taken place in Darwen on New Year's Day, 1876. Partick were the far superior team and won 7–0. This made no stir at the time, but to Darwen it must have been a yardstick, and when eighteen months later they had improved and wanted to measure themselves again, it was to Partick that they turned. Their friendship with the Scots club was interesting and could improve their game. But neither they nor anyone else realised at this stage its momentousness.

Tommy Marshall

In January 1877 the *Darwen News* reported a 'Campanological Entertainment' by local hand-bell ringers, and the Orchard Mill Fire Brigade Supper, paid for by the Walsh family at the Greenway Arms. Both received more column inches than a game in the snow between Darwen Reserves and a factory team, and another between two factory teams that was shortened by rain. So did the Annual Report of the Free Library Committee (borrowings had risen and 435 new volumes been purchased) and the Literary Society's plans to hear a paper on the poet Chatterton. Football was covered, but it was not yet major news. On 10 February Darwen won 1–0 against Church, a village team, with a goal by James Knowles, and in March there are reports of games between four different mill or foundry teams, one of them from Blackburn.

The *Darwen News* had been founded in 1874 as the voice of the Liberal masters, and although it rumbles on about Disraeli's imperialist foreign policy its increased coverage of leisure activities reveals more about immediate lives: the professional Theatre Royal opened with an interesting programme, in April there was a Three Day Walking Match for professionals in the Agricultural Hall, and in May the first concert of the Darwen Musical Union, sponsored by Shorrocks and Ashtons and Walshes, at which the soprano wives of the elite received standing ovations.

When the cricket season opened, the Barley Bank pavilion was redecorated and given additional seating for ladies. James and George Walsh, W. T. Walsh, Thomas Duxbury and the club professional, Crookes, all played in the opening practice match, and we begin to see mentions of working-class sporting talent. Moorhouse and R. Kirkham were youngsters who would play soccer against Old Etonians, and so was John Duxbury, younger brother of Thomas. In June there were 'two days of cricket, music and fun' with The Clowns, a showbusiness eleven who used cricket in the afternoon to advertise their concerts at night, and James, George and Charles Walsh all played in midweek games against Werneth, near Oldham, and Stonyhurst College. In July, James Walsh played for the Singles, and W. T. Walsh for the Marrieds, and on 25 August the Cricket and Football Club held its Annual Athletic Festival and Gala, which saw the arrival of a crucial football talent.

Tommy Marshall was nineteen years old, born in the nearby hamlet of Withnell and working as a loomer in John Walmsley's Lodge Bank Mill. This paid him £40 a year, to which he hoped to add his winnings as a professional sprinter. Shortish, powerful, balanced, with a square, cocky and determined face and a moustache trimmed to a downturn, he must have joined to play football because he does not figure at cricket. He was to be a personality player, one of the first northern workmen to play for England, and his pace and cool head could make the difference. He showed both in the Gala. In the hundred-yards sprint for members he ran from scratch and won. His prize was a cricket bag. And in the hundred-yards professional handicap he had seven yards' start and took the first prize of £5. Over the next three years, until the handicapper beat him, he won place money in several similar events. In the four- or five-a-side football tournaments that were a feature of all the late-summer Lancashire galas he was successful for longer, and shared many first and second prizes; and he would surely have placed bets on himself. That his training routines helped the football team can be deduced from the fact that in several key matches they were to show better condition than their opponents.

At the end of September Darwen's cricketers beat Burnley in a return grudge match at Barley Bank. George Walsh made 67 and hit two balls into a garden adjoining the ground. In the final event of the cricket season the first eleven played with broomsticks (shades of Harrow house yards) against the second, who used bats. The twenty-year-old Abraham Hayes played for the seconds. He was a weaver and when the football season started was the team's regular centre forward alongside John Lewis. Lewis was born in Market Drayton in Shropshire in 1855. In 1868, after the death of his preacher father, he moved to Blackburn and was apprenticed to his brother-in-law's coach-building business. There is no evidence that he ever attended the grammar school but his friend Arthur

Constantine did, and in 1875 the pair were instrumental in the foundation of Blackburn Rovers.

In those days men flitted between clubs to get a game, and until local rivalries hotted up Lewis was happy to turn out for Darwen. A friend of Tom Hindle, he was also courting a Darwen girl named Alice Kay, and subsequently married her. He was a bustling and active forward, said the Almanacks, but unlucky with injuries. He was a thinker about the game, and became an outstanding referee: he was to take charge of three FA Cup and two Olympic Games Finals, the last in Antwerp in 1920 when he was sixty-five years old. In 2003 Blackburn Rovers paid to have his gravestone restored.

W. T. Walsh was said to be Darwen's best soccer player, but in October he broke his leg in a game against Church and never played again. Despite this misfortune, the team held good form and resolution. When the chairman, Thomas Duxbury, the half-back and secretary, Tom Hindle, and the crippled captain, W. T. Walsh, looked around they believed that there was no better team on the local horizon. But how could they move on? There was only one way, which hitherto no Lancashire team had shown the nerve or the finances to take, and that was to enter the Football Association Cup Competition. Now, in the late autumn of 1876, two Lancashire clubs took the plunge, Darwen and the middle-class Manchester Association.

They were among forty-three hopeful entrants, of whom Glasgow's Queen's Park withdrew before the competition started. Of the remainder only seven teams were based outside the south of England: Sheffield, Nottingham, Darwen, Manchester Association, Druids, Shropshire Wanderers and Grantham. There were the two universities, four school or old boy teams, and three regimentals. The rest were from London and its surrounds, the furthest afield being from towns like High Wycombe and Reading. Regimental teams contained some other ranks among officers who had played at their schools, but Darwen were the only side to have a preponderance of actual uneducated working men. The mere fact of their entry made the *Darwen News* sit up and take notice. There was public interest and there was circulation value, and the first match to receive a massive increase in coverage, even though the paper did not send its own reporter but cobbled together a piece from accounts in the Glasgow papers, was November's return game against Partick.

Coasting Shirts

Partick is on the north bank of the Clyde and at the beginning of the nineteenth century it was a village of thatched cottages, an old ruined castle, clear water in the Kelvin River, and a few weavers and watermills. It was a subject for Glasgow watercolourists, and a favourite destination for a weekend jaunt. Its subsequent industrial expansion was as dramatic as that of Darwen, except that Partick became part of a city. There were weaving sheds, grain mills, bleaching works, engineering and ship-building: in 1835 Tod and McGregor's yard launched *La Plata*, the world's first all-iron steamer.

When Kirkham arrived he would have heard Gaelic and Irish on the streets as well as the languages of foreign sailors: Glasgow was a melting pot that attracted a huge influx of people from Ireland and the Scottish Highlands, and Partick was in the middle of a building boom. Four-storey tenements were rising everywhere and there was no longer a gap between what had been the village and the city. A hundred and forty trains a day ran through Partick between Glasgow and Clydebank, and as many trams went up and down Argyle Street. Working-class tenements swarmed with people and living conditions were squalid. A feature of the 1871 Scottish Census is that it lists the number of windowed rooms per household. Most had two but many had only one. There were wall-beds, cold water, outside sanitation and eight households per block. Kirkham would have lodged in something similar, or in a pub if he felt flush.

At the same time Glasgow was a world city. It had noble neo-classical edifices and an educated merchant class that was about to produce a generation of painters and collectors. The architect Charles Rennie Mackintosh was born there in 1868, and in 1876 the fifteen-year-old William Burrell, who was to form one of the world's great collections of Impressionist and early modern paintings, and leave it to the city, started work in his father's shipping agency.

The local *Partick Observer* may have complained that just across the river Govan was 'maintaining its unenviable reputation as the haunt of criminals', and that among the Irish there was 'a notorious character named Nancy Sloan', but it also advertised 'Coasting Shirts to be worn at the coast on holiday', and its lengthy articles about Chinese river steamboats (built in Govan) and what the death of Cardinal Altonelli might mean for Vatican politics reflected global concerns. And, like the *Darwen News*, it had begun to include football coverage.

Queen's Park

The story of how soccer started in Scotland is the story of Queen's Park, and it is a romantic one, of young men who left the Highlands to find work in Glasgow's offices and warehouses, and who met every week to do athletics. They lived around the southern edge of the city, in respectable suburbs, where they lost their usual plot of land to new building, and went to the public park instead. There they met youths who lodged at the YMCA hostel opposite and played kickabout football. Jumpers and discarded clothing were indeed goalposts when in July 1867 the Highland men were drawn into the kickabout, and enjoyed it so much that they decided to form a club.

They debated what to call themselves: The Northern, Celts or Morayshire, where they came from. They settled on Queen's Park, after the place where they kicked about, and could store their gear in the Deaf and Dumb Institute. Their entrance fee was a shilling and the annual subscription sixpence, and the first money went at once on the purchase of a ball. They sent off to Lillywhite's in London for a copy of the FA Rules, which they altered a little to suit their own ideas. At first they played soccer in summer and rugby in winter, because they could get a rugby game against Glasgow Academicals and the other Scottish versions of old boy and public school teams.

Interestingly, the first Scottish attempt at an organised football club had been made by an Edinburgh lawyer in 1824, but there were too few people for it to catch on: it did so through the new English-style public schools, who because they could play on fields took to a handling, carrying and body-tackling game.

All this invites an interesting question. It is: where had the youths who lodged at the YMCA and kicked about in the park learned football? What was their kickabout like? Did it allow handling? Come to that, did Darwen lunchtime mill boys in the 1840s? One day, we must hope, researchers will give us the answers.

At first Queen's Park themselves played matches among the members. Teams were picked on the field and there might be fifteen or twenty a side. They wore different-coloured nightcaps as colours. By 1869 there were forty playing members and they would undertake what we might call missionary journeys to show people soccer, when they would stop in the middle of a game to explain what they were doing. They refused to play teams who wanted to carry the ball, hack, handle, body-tackle and score from touchdowns, and progress was slow. In 1870 they played five games against outside opponents, and in 1871/2 could only manage three.

Some of the Queen's Park players lived in the same lodgings and two, the Smith brothers, went to work in London, where they played for South Norwood and even represented that club at meetings of the English FA. It was this contact with Robert Smith in particular that enabled Charles W. Alcock, by now secretary of the Football Association as well as editor of the *Football Annual*, to set up the first unofficial international match between England and Scots living in London. This was played at Kennington Oval in December 1871, and was followed by two similar exhibition matches. Alcock, inspired throughout, no doubt, by the fact that there had already been a formal rugby international, now wrote an open letter to the *Glasgow Herald* inviting gentlemen from Scotland to arrange a more official encounter.

Queen's Park responded, and after the match they joined the Football Association and committed themselves to play soccer in the winter. In 1873 they adopted their celebrated black and white hooped shirts, and were the prime movers in the formation of the Scottish Football Association.

Rapid progress ensued. Representative Glasgow teams played annually against Sheffield, whose offside and throw-in laws were similar. Queen's Park themselves went to London, Nottingham, Birmingham, Stoke, Cambridge University and Manchester, where in April 1878 they were watched by Tom Hindle and John Lewis of Darwen. Rangers and Ayr Thistle also travelled. In 1872 there had been ten Scottish clubs. By 1876 there were thirty-five in Glasgow alone, and, like Partick, these were fully fledged members of the Scottish FA, beneath and beyond whom was a proliferation of local and working-class teams.

Partick itself had been a rugby club called Clydebank, and had a winter rent on a cricket club ground and pavilion in Inchview Park. Trams passed the ground every seven minutes, and this easy access explains why it was chosen as the venue for the first international in 1872. In the same year the club took up soccer, and almost certainly became more working class.

Because early football coverage depended on club secretaries sending in their reports, the *Partick Observer* can be a patchy guide to the local scene, but it is clear that below the level of Partick itself there was very lively activity. Local entries for the Glasgow Public Parks Cup Competition included Partick Academy, Partickhill, Partick Ramblers, Partick Violet and Kelvinside. If these have a somewhat middle-class ring to them, other clubs mentioned in the paper hint at street names, pubs and the origins of their immigrant founders: Stonefield, Our Boys, Dewdrop, Gangforward, Govan Union, Glencoe, Langlands, Pikeshill, Possil Blue Bell. There were also Post Office and factory teams, particularly in Govan. Even allowing for population differences, there seem to be many more clubs than sprang up in Darwen.

Darwen, however, had experienced continuity. Three successive generations of the Walsh family could have watched or played in folk football, its thirty- and thirteen-a-side reductions, street and mill yard kickabouts, pub contests, Harrow Footer and Association rules. Players in the Glasgow melting pot had no such history in their veins. They had no traditions, and that is why they changed the game.

The Scots passing game

There can be no doubt that the Queen's Park passing game, which soon became the Scots passing game, was original in its day and a decisive idea in the history of football. But what was it like, actually, and what did the players think they were doing? Today we are used to journalism and TV punditry that discuss tactics and formations in great detail, and we are all more or less aware that most modern tactics are devised to counter earlier tactics, which were themselves devised to counter even earlier tactics. For example, in the 1950s the withdrawn centre forward was used against the stopper centre half, and in recent seasons 4–4–2 Premiership formations have become a more fluid 4–3–3.

When Queen's Park played scratch games among themselves they played football that had emerged, via the FA Rules, from the public school and other dilutions of the folk football free-for-all. Had any of them even seen soccer, in London or anywhere else? Probably not, although they possibly saw Scottish public school handling games. But they had no emotional baggage and no knowledge, particularly, of how the free-for-all had become the chase-about in which they found themselves. Etonian Field Game players could refer in the mid-1870s to how their game had been played decades earlier, and there must have been many old chaps in Darwen pubs who saw the Tottington encounters, and played in six-a-side pub games thereafter. The founders of Queen's Park, who until about 1874 were still the chief players, saw merely the game as it existed, and they invented things off the field as well as on. Not for them the urbane casualness of chaps around London who played for one club at weekends and another in midweek. Members of Queen's Park were never allowed to play against the club without permission, and they elected a captain and gave him as absolute power over team matters as a top modern manager. One of them, the goalkeeper Hugh Gardner, gave his men cards on which he had written their position and duties.

In folk football the tactical essence was the ball itself. The violence was to get opponents away from the ball, and to protect the passage of the man carrying or kicking it. In 1830 some Darwen men stood back to block a breakaway rush, and others slightly apart to start one: but the focus was the melee around the ball, and the same was true of Westminster Greens, Harrow Footer and the Eton Wall Game.

What happened in Westminster Fields and in soccer itself was that the chase continued but with less violence. There was no body-tackling, but what a *Scottish F.A. Handbook* defined as 'that scientific jerk of the shoulder which removes a player off the ball' could be used against men not in possession, including the goalkeeper. Bumping and banging forwards rushed to the ball and scrimmages could be prolonged and messy.

In today's rugby union a scrimmage around a tackled man is an opportunity for one side to halt an attack and try to regain possession, and for the other to draw in defenders and go wide. This is exactly how the scrimmage operated in early soccer. People would link arms and try to keep the ball among their own feet until there was an opportunity for a runner. When someone broke there was a wild pursuit and if the runner was checked his 'backer-up' would attempt to continue. If the ball was lost more backers-up were needed, to get the ball stuck in another scrimmage and try to recover it. Overall, wrote men like Alcock, backing up was vital.

Chase and scrimmage was soccer's first tactical pattern, and the Scots passing game was the second. It tried to get the ball around the melee and to hold a more measured possession long enough to score. There is some journalistic evidence to show how this was done, but before we look at it there is another point that is worth recalling and it is to do with people's physical development. In the 1790s people around Darwen had been described as 'a tall, florid and comely race', but when the team came to play southern gentlemen in the 1870s, generations of poor industrial living conditions had made them smaller than their opponents. At a time when weight in the scrimmage was a crucial issue in football the more privileged social classes were for the most part taller, heavier and faster than other people. Queen's Park may well have been influenced by their experiences against posh English sides to find a way around this disadvantage, as they seem to have been by their games against sturdy rough-and-tumble Scots rural teams like Vale of Leven and the Highland side Drummond.

Again, the need to avoid injuries when men had to go to work to earn a living was an explicit point of debate in the 1863 meeting that set up the English Football Association, and a reason why the majority, having voted against handling, went on to ban hacking and body-tackling. Injuries were certainly why clubs like Turton and Darwen gave up mixed rules and played soccer from the mid-1870s, so Queen's Park, whose members were serious about their workday responsibilities, may well have trimmed both their rules and their style of play in ways that favoured skill and discounted violence.

At the same time, it would be a mistake to think that the way they played was a 'beautiful game' in the modern sense. They did not move the ball around like Tottenham in 1950 or Barcelona in the 2000s. They never envisaged our football. What they sought was to make more sense of what they had, and in doing this they were like Harrow schoolmasters influenced by notions of sport as a physical trial and moral force.

The 1876/7 *Scottish F.A. Handbook* says that an Association's function was to 'develop football as a game and to render it as perfect as possible'. This would 'conduce materially to the maintenance of that superiority of British nerve and muscle that played no unimportant part in shaping the history of the world'. This is a blunt statement, and a more embracing one than Harrovian quasi-religious metaphor: it boasts that all Britons were superior to the rest of the world, and not just the elite.

Having noted this, let us consider the newspaper evidence.

How teams line up can reveal how they play, and this was the case in the earliest games between the English and the Scots. A fundamental moment in soccer was the 1870 definition of the goalkeeper as the one man allowed to handle the ball, and English teams then lined up in what we might call a folk-football-inspired formation of a goalkeeper, defenders and scrimmagers, of whom the fastest men played wide. In the first proper international, at Inchview in 1872, the English played a 1–1–1–8 formation and were said to be faster, two stones a man heavier, and to have applied constant pressure. The Scots were saved by their 1–2–2–6 formation, where men lying back stopped the rushes, and by the fact that 'they played excellently well together'. A year later, in the 1873 international at Kennington Oval, the Scots picked several men who lived in London, seemingly because it saved travel money. The consequence, said the *Glasgow Herald*, was that the Scots centre forwards could not rely on their outsides, who had learned to play in England.

What does this mean? How exactly did Scots-trained men play together? A report in the *Partick Observer* of 10 March 1877 gives us vivid answers. And as luck would have it, this one detailed description of a passing system that I have come across is about men who were fundamental to the story of the Darwen underdogs.

The match was at Inchview and Partick beat the 1st Lanark Rifle Volunteers 5–1. Partick's two right-wing forwards were Fergus Suter and W. Kirkham, and the paper describes Suter 'dodging those who attempted to stop his progress, every now and then passing to Kirkham, who was a little in advance. Thus nearing the goal he would centre.' Two goals ensued when they varied the play: once Kirkham ran through and scored himself, and later he had a shot handled by a defender. In 1877 there were no penalty kicks, and a goal could not be scored direct from a normal free kick; but from Kirkham's kick 'a severe scrimmage ensued, resulting in the ball being carried through'.

It is clear from later descriptions that Kirkham was a very skilful dribbler, and by 'dodging', a frequent phrase in accounts of the period, something like feints and body-swerves, as opposed to ball tricks, is presumably what is meant. But the key thing one feels is that Kirkham was slightly in advance, instead of backing up from behind. The fault of the English-reared outside men in 1873 was that they hung behind the man in possession in the hope that when he lost control they could accelerate on to the loose ball and launch their own solo dribble; or, if that was not possible, form a scrimmage.

In contrast, the sort of combination invented by Queen's Park and essayed by Suter and Kirkham meant that the other forwards could play in much more of a line, and hope for the ball to come to

them when they had a sight of goal. Also, in a
1–2–2–6 formation the two backs and two halves
would be able to support and pass to one another,
instead of having few options beyond a dribble or a
big kick ahead. Play became less scrappy, more
thoughtful and incidentally more aesthetic. Not, we
may suspect, that this was the original intention. The
original idea is much more likely to have been defensive: that it was easier to stop a rush with men who
faced it than by overtaken men who ran to catch up.

Of course, the English offside law stated that when
the ball was kicked forward a player must have three
opponents ahead of him, and this is why attackers
hung back. But for a few vital years the Scots law
was different: a man was offside not when the ball
was kicked but when it reached him. This must have
made it easier to play in a line instead of a pack with
a spearhead, and given players the confidence to hold
away from the ball a little, and to run ahead in
anticipation of a pass. It may well have been the
thing that made the difference.

Dutch carpenters

To Kirkham and Suter, young men in work and enjoying their football, life must have been fun: but in fact by 1877 the economic situation was not good. Britain's industries were no longer unrivalled. The world's economy was shifting in favour of Germany and America. Competition for raw materials increased and costs rose. Wages were under pressure. Workers like the Blackburn weavers had in the early 1850s negotiated piece-work settlements that held for two decades. Women cotton operatives won Saturday half-days in 1850 and in the early 1870s it became general for men, which was certainly the biggest factor in the spread of football as an East Lancashire spectator sport. But now a long period of prosperity was facing challenges. At the end of 1877 the London *Times* calculated that the year had seen 191 strikes, with the building trades, iron and metal, and coalminers the worst affected.

For the present Darwen kept working, but in Glasgow trouble began in the shipyards, and in March 1877 Partick had played a charity match for Govan Poor Relief. In April, Partick shipwrights struck for better rates, the work of other trades was held up, and some voted to strike themselves. In May the owners of most yards declared a lockout, which presumably put the Partick footballer, and shipyard worker and future Darwen star, Jimmy Love out of work. 'No honest worker,' said the *Partick Observer* in its support for the bosses, 'will refuse to be paid in proportion to his work. It is the scamping loafer who fears payment by results.'

In June the Inglis yard brought in Dutch carpenters to finish the vessels lying on its stocks. A week later the local construction boom collapsed. Tenements had been run up ahead of demand and several builders went bankrupt. Some shipyards resumed work at the end of July, after the Glasgow Fair Holidays, but arbitration disputes dragged on into October, as more trades were forced back to work at the old rates. Did the construction collapse put the young stonemason Fergus Suter out of work? Impossible to know, and he was not in the Partick sides that played the old season's final matches in April, and the new one's first games in the autumn. Did he go away to seek work? Lose his form? Suffer an injury? Or was he taking time to adjust to the fact that when he reappeared in the team it was not as a forward but as a fullback?

Handsomely defeated

Darwen arranged fixtures with Partick to expand their horizons, and discover how good or deficient they were, and what they needed to do to improve. This was despite the fact that Partick themselves were not one of Scotland's best teams. No Partick men appear in any of the *Scottish F.A. Handbook* lists of principal players; it might even be that the accident of Kirkham's presence gave the club ambitions that it could not fulfil, and that the rent of Inchview Park was an obligation that became hard to meet. When the team disbanded in 1885 the lease was taken over by their successors Thistle, now Partick Thistle, who were backed by local small businesses.

Nevertheless, when Darwen went to Inchview for a return game they were 'handsomely defeated' 5–0 on a very bad pitch, and the manner of the loss was as cruel a lesson as the scoreline. The *Glasgow Herald* and the *North British Daily Mail* joined in the view that the match was very one-sided. Partick went ahead on the half-hour, when after a forward pass from a halfback the Partick forward Wilson shot and Darwen's goalkeeper, Booth, let the ball go through his hands. Ten minutes later Partick were three up, through Muirhead and W. Kirkham. Darwen retaliated with a four-man folk-football-style rush but Partick's backs got the ball away 'before the rest of the Englishmen' came up. In the second half Muirhead made it 4–0 when four men inter-passed after a scrimmage, and Wilson scored a fifth just before the end.

Darwen were good individually, said the press, but did not play well together. As the game went against them 'they became rather confused'. The backs were too far back and the forwards too far forward. This is a common fault to this day, and often happens because defenders who are losing pace lie too deep. Maybe this befell the ageing Darwen fullback McWetherill and compounded the defeat. Partick's backs, in contrast, showed how to support their forwards. They clearly played frequent and accurate balls to the wings, who themselves put in quite long centres, a sort of play that over the next eighteen months came to characterise Darwen themselves. Fergus Suter, fast, a good dodger and a precise kicker, was fundamental to this, as he was to Partick on the day; people had begun to realise that the men who could influence the tempo and direction of the play were not those in the forward pack, but the ones behind them, backs like Suter and halves like his friend and Partick colleague Hugh McIntyre. And, indeed, like James Knowles of Darwen when he later dropped back from the forwards.

For the record Darwen's team was Booth; Duxbury; McWetherill; Crookes; Hindle; Marshall; R. Kirkham; Knowles; Lewis; Hayes; Bury.

Blue and French grey

Defeat in Partick did not demoralise Darwen. They were determined to improve and their ambitions were high: had they done any worse than Nottingham Forest, who had just been beaten 6–2 by Queen's Park? They thought not, and before the end of November lived up to their estimation of themselves and beat Blackburn Rovers 4–0. The rough state of the ground made good dribbling impossible, and Rovers, who had not at this stage played very many games, showed little combination. There were a thousand spectators, John Lewis played on this occasion for Blackburn, and Darwen's goals came from Bury, Knowles, Hayes, who tapped in a rebound from the post, and Bury again. Rovers were the one team Darwen had failed to beat in 1876/7, and the result must have seemed to justify the Darwen Committee's decision to raise their sights and enter the FA Cup. Queen's Park had entered before, of course, and Sheffield, but so far no one from Lancashire. Now the Manchester Association entered as well, and Darwen drew them at home in a regional First Round.

In modern times Manchester and Liverpool have been two of the strongest soccer centres in the world, but early progress was slow. What was needed for clubs to spring up was men with both free time and a shared sense of identity. In Liverpool low-paid casual dock work, and none for women and juveniles, created a much poorer and more alienated culture than that of the cotton towns; there were more religious divisions and fewer working-class organisations, and casual trades didn't win the Saturday half-day until much later.

In Manchester there were various clubs but most of them were for middle-class men who favoured rugby rules, and again it took time for the engineering trades, which had overtaken cotton manufacture in the city's economy, to get their half-days. The Manchester Association itself had been formed in 1875. It had eighty members, compared to Darwen's fifty, and a ground in the one-time village and now lower-middle-class suburb Eccles. The team's colours were blue and French grey.

The tie was played in good weather but the turf was a bit spongy. The crowd was the biggest so far in Darwen. Bookmakers and newspapers pundits seem to have expected Manchester to win but two of their players arrived late and the game began without them. Before they arrived John Lewis, back again from Blackburn, headed Darwen into the lead, and went on to score two more goals, one disputed, against one disallowed for Manchester. 'Disputed' means that the umpires disagreed, and the referee could or would not decide. The Darwen team was Booth; J. Duxbury; McWetherill; T. Hindle; J. Hayes; J. Knowles; J. Lewis; T. Bury;

R. Crookes; R. Kirkham; T. Marshall. This line-up does not put men in their usual positions, and J. Hayes was the brother of A. Hayes. But if it is how they played it is the only time that Marshall was wide on the left.

This victory was followed by a positive triumph on New Year's Day 1878, when Partick paid their return visit. Darwen played their Cup eleven and Partick had Suter at right back and captain, his older brother Edward in goal, Jimmy Love at halfback and among the forwards their Secretary, John Gloag, and W. Kirkham.

There was a crowd of 3,000, many of them women who were admitted free. It cost extra to sit on lined-up brewery wagons. The pitch was in a very bad state, mud being ankle-deep, but the play was very fast and when Darwen went ahead spectators threw 'their hats sticks and umbrellas into the air with a seeming disregard for their property', said the *Darwen News*. In the second half Partick had the wind behind them, and numerous shots at goal, but were kept out by 'superb back play' and 'magnificent goalkeeping'.

Jimmy Love did make it 1–1 with a screw kick, but the game turned again when Darwen scored three quick goals to lead 4–1: for the last Marshall made the most wonderful run to beat Suter one on one, which would not be the last fiery moment between these two. When Marshall shot, the ball stuck in the mud and he had to go on again to score. At that Darwen thought the game was over, but Partick scored again so the game finished 4-2.

Next day Partick went to Blackburn, where the Rovers beat them 2–1 in the first match at their new Alexandra Meadows ground. Gate receipts were £25 6s 0d., which did not quite cover expenses; presumably Partick required a guarantee.

New Year's Day had been a Tuesday and on the Saturday Darwen entertained Sheffield in the Second Round of the Cup, a confrontation which seems a good moment at which to ask an interesting question.

Sheffield

That question is: why did professional football begin in the cotton towns of East Lancashire and not among the steelworks of industrial Sheffield? After all, organised club football had a longer history in Sheffield than in Lancashire, and longer, even, than around London. Sheffield FC was started in 1855, when of its fifty-seven original members one had been to Rugby but seventeen to the local Collegiate School. They were the sons of local business and professional men and they picked scratch teams from the membership. They sent off to Rugby and Winchester for copies of their rules and by 1862, when they published their own, had arrived at a non-handling, non body-tackling game with no offside.

In 1866 Sheffield played their first game in London, for which a one-man offside rule was agreed, and in 1867, lesser local clubs having sprung up, Sheffield members took the lead in the formation of the Sheffield Association.

Both heading and the referee's use of a whistle seem to have been invented in Sheffield, and in 1871 the Sheffield Association joined the FA. Every year between 1874 and 1879 they played representative Glasgow Elevens. The Sheffield Club entered the FA

Cup as early as the 1873/4 season, and although they scratched once, in other years they were only narrowly beaten by the top teams Clapham Rovers, Wanderers and Royal Engineers. Then they stood still.

Reports of the 1877 game against Glasgow indicate that Sheffield used a long kick and chase tactics, and, although Sheffield Wednesday had a good Cup run in 1882, the city's teams did not reach a higher playing level or enjoy big success until the mid-1890s.

A fundamental reason for this is the attitude of the original Sheffield club, and of its members who controlled the local Association. When the club sought outside fixtures it preferred to meet the middle-class likes of Notts County, Nottingham Forest and Lincoln, and during the 1860s actually gave up matches against teams in Sheffield itself: it objected to the way in which these teams would borrow good men from other clubs. This attitude was detrimental to overall quality because football in Sheffield was self-contained. Its clubs did not represent separate townships with ancient rivalries and assertions of identity, like Darwen and Tottington and Blackburn. There was not the same competitiveness, and it is indicative that it was music hall owners and not the clubs themselves who thought up the knock-out competitions of 1867 and 1868. Three thousand people paid threepence each to see Hallam beat Norfolk in the 1867 final, but the promoters kept the money and the Sheffield club itself neither entered nor exposed other locals to its high-level playing experience.

During the 1860s the Sheffield Association opposed the payment of expenses for time lost at work, and when the moment came they both opposed professionalism and resented the fact that their attitude curtailed their own playing success. The leader of these men was the redoubtable J. C. Clegg. A local solicitor born in 1850, Clegg had been a considerable athlete, running a hundred yards in evens, and played for England in the 1872 international against Scotland at Partick's Inchview ground. In later years, when he was the FA's most powerful administrator, he claimed to remember little about it. 'None of the southern amateurs spoke to me,' he said, 'so I wouldn't play again.'

Clegg resented what he saw as the snobbery of the public school men. He was to nurse his hurt provincial pride, and when the time came he took his revenge. At the other end of the social scale he disliked the working-class footballers for different reasons. His public utterances against professionalism were the routine ones: it would encourage drink, give power to betting men and bookmakers, and somehow pollute the game. In Clegg's case, however, I think his opposition was really inspired by something deeper in his nature and in his experience. In a sense it was something both more moral and less moralising: his reaction to the so-called Sheffield Outrages of 1866.

At even so late a date in Britain's industrialisation, the Sheffield cutlery trades were organised according to a medieval system of small workshops, masters, craftsmen and apprentices. The masters strove to make this system more capitalistic, and the workers opposed them. In 1866, after decades of poisonous industrial relations, the workers turned to violence. There were numerous bombings and shootings, for which no one was punished because no one would give evidence, and in 1867 the government imposed a Royal Commission. It sat in Sheffield and guaranteed witnesses immunity from prosecution.

Disraeli's plan was not to punish people, but to expose the Outrages, draw a line under them, and clear the ground for the future. His tactic succeeded because both workmen and employers sought to justify themselves, and to improve their situations: they confessed what they had done and explained why they had done it. The result was that the Commission recommended, and the Government introduced, legislation that laid the basis for all subsequent trade union law, and was a decisive step forward.

But the fact was that working men had literally got away with murder, and with other serious crimes against both persons and property, and the middle classes did not like it. J. C. Clegg was seventeen and a trainee solicitor, a young man who believed in the law but saw it set aside for political expedience. May not this explain a great deal about him?

Beyond doubt the middle-class men who ran Sheffield football were not friendly to the advancement within the game of working people. They refused broken-time payments and benefit matches, when in Lancashire benefits were common, and match day expenses seem to have been paid from the start; and whereas members of the Sheffield club would not play lower-class teams, in Lancashire the Kays and Walshes gave up their Harrow rules to please ordinary people. Whatever this says, if anything, about a narrower provinciality in one place than in the other, the fact is that in Sheffield there were real explosions, but not football ones.

Soiled kid gloves

Despite this, in January 1878 Sheffield were not yet perceived to have stagnated, and Lancashire football had not quite boomed. Most people in the south would have reckoned Sheffield to be the strongest provincial side. In the previous Cup campaign they had beaten South Norwood 7–0 and lost only 1–0 to Royal Engineers, and in the current competition had just knocked out Nottingham Forest by a convincing 3–0. When they realised that the weather would be cold in Darwen they arrived with a job lot of soiled white kid gloves that had previously been worn by guests at a ball or a concert.

W. Kirkham, who on New Year's Day had played for Partick, now appeared for Darwen, and must have left his job in Glasgow. He made a brilliant early run but was not supported, all the Darwen players being too near their own goal. Kirkham danced about to keep possession and one Sheffield player seemed about to hit him. The crowd booed, feeling turned bad, and the match ended in one of those incidents which on the one hand bemuse the modern reader, and on the other remind us that there is not much in football that is new.

In March 1878 the *Partick Observer* would report a controversy over a match in which the local team, Glencoe, had walked off sooner than play against the wind. Here Darwen went behind, but protested that the Sheffield scorer was offside. The umpires failed to agree and the referee, from Blackburn, allowed the goal to stand. His behaviour, said the *Darwen News* 'was in singularly bad taste to say the least'.

Darwen refused to play on and the players left the field to wash and dress, Sheffield going to the Smalley's Arms pub, where they had tea. Tom Hindle, twenty-three years old, Darwen secretary and a player in the match, wrote a letter of protest to the Football Association, but to no avail. The result was confirmed and Darwen were out. Sheffield reached the Fourth Round, where they lost 3–0 to the eventual winners, Wanderers.

A week later Darwen went to Blackburn Rovers, taking a large number of supporters with them, but could only draw 0–0, Marshall wasting a chance to win by shooting wide from a good position. The Barley Bank pitch was now in such bad condition that the last home game of the season against Eagley was played 'on a field opposite the residence of W. Almond Esq.' The players had to change in outhouses, instead of the usual Greenway Arms. The result was a 2–2 draw that led to newspaper criticism of the team, and to controversy.

Communicated

'Communicated' is the word used by the *Darwen News* to indicate a report sent in by a club secretary or other member, and since Tom Hindle was a player and is criticised, it is improbable that he was the communicator of this particular and inflammatory match report. Was the author W. T. Walsh, then, the captain who would never play again because of his broken leg, and a year later wrote a blunt and amusing letter asking for travel money to play Old Etonians? Was it J. J. Riley, flexing his muscles as a freelance before the launch of his own sports paper? Was it the committee chairman, Thomas Duxbury? Or could it have been the would-be literary man, James Christopher Ashton?

One inclines towards Ashton, somehow, because Riley's style is professional: Riley had a role in the community, from which he was able to criticise without giving personal offence. But here, as in the paper's later account of the team's first trip to London, there are flowery touches and names are named. There is the tone of someone who has no direct responsibility for events or for keeping people happy, but is sure of what should be done. An educated amateur's outspokenness, as it were. Someone unafraid to put himself forward and say what others had thought but had been careful not to express in so many words.

Whoever the communicator was, he began by accusing Eagley of importing players from Turton, Egerton and Bolton, and of playing for a draw, which they got; partly because of the selfishness of some of the Darwen players, 'a want of united play', and partly because some Darwen regulars were missing. Eagley had won the toss, played with the wind, and begun with a rush. After five minutes they scored a soft goal and a minute later Darwen equalised. Six minutes later Eagley scored again and Darwen did not make it 2–2 until the eightieth minute. The criticisms of Darwen's defenders were outspoken by contemporary standards. Since conceding five goals to Partick, goalkeeper Booth 'has shown an excess of nervous timidity. The only thing he can now manage is a slashing kick from a place kick.' Right back Duxbury made sorry misses that led to the goals, and left back Crookes was 'wretched'. Hindle lacked spirit and dash and the team's only tactic seemed to be to pass to Marshall on the right wing. Marshall centred well, and Bury met them with his head, but 'we think it is a hobby-horse ridden too much'. All the forwards were inclined to be too selfish. At one point three of them faced the Eagley goalkeeper when he was two yards from his line but none of them barged him, and he dodged his way clear.

At that time each team supplied an umpire, to whom the players appealed for fouls, and the referee, supposedly a neutral, would only be involved if the umpires disagreed. The abuses and flaws of this system can be as comic as they were frequent. In a match between Queen's Park and Vale of Leven in December 1876, reported the *Scottish Football Annual*, 'a shot from Weir, straight for goal, struck the umbrella of one of the umpires, and the chance was lost'. In that instance the referee did award the goal, and umbrellas seem to have been as much to signal with as to keep off the rain.

Here the Eagley umpire 'did not understand his business, or if he did was not eager to adhere to it, for we several times saw him giving instructions to his man how and where to play . . .' Nor did he wait for appeals against Darwen, but gave 'hands' and fouls without being asked. Disputes were thus 'the unpleasantest feature of the game', and even the Darwen umpire was not blameless. He stood still and did not follow the ball. Players ran into him and the ball hit him. Eagley were offside seven times, and scored from it once, but it was never disputed because the umpire was too far away.

The report ends with a spin-doctoring flourish. Thirty-three years ago Darwen was famous for both football and honesty. When 'we compete with the surrounding towns in billiards or band contests, football or cricket, we invariably play our own man instead of scouring the country for strangers to help us'. Even so, the team has done splendidly, and been a credit to the town. The propaganda tone and the local pride are interesting, and were to be echoed in Walsh's letter a year later, and whatever memory of 1845 football is evoked the actual subtext is clear. Rebuilding is required. We need new and better men in several positions.

Which is what happened, of course. Never mind being famous for honesty: and were they, actually, or did they just like to believe that they were? The fact was that unlike a boarding house at Harrow, which must pick from its pupils, or a regimental or university team, or a club that put up unspoken social barriers, Darwen were free to recruit and team-build, and proceeded to do so. They shifted some men, promoted others, scoured the locality and acquired the first professionals. 'Communicated' in the *Darwen News* of 1878 is where modern football ruthlessness began.

A benefit for W. T. Walsh

After the Eagley game some of the Darwen players took part in minor fixtures for other teams, and in a match in which a scratch team of Blackburn Lawyers beat Darwen Rovers 1–0 'innate selfishness was displayed as a fully developed acquirement by some of the Darwen first team'. Such criticism was also a polemic in favour of the passing game, and seems to have whipped up public interest.

One thousand people went on a special train from Darwen to Turton for a match that was actually a benefit for 'our worthy captain Mr W. T. Walsh', who twenty-one weeks after his injury was still off work and had a young wife and family. At Turton station the staff were overwhelmed by the numbers arriving, and three or four of them stood in the road below the station collecting tickets in their pockets and caps, and with both hands full. At Chapeltown village the crowd amused itself by throwing the corpse of a huge rat at each other's heads.

The weather was fine and the pitch was in excellent condition, but twenty yards bigger than the maximum allowed by the laws of the game, a hangover from when Turton played Harrow-style rules. Darwen had striven to find a neutral referee and

Turton had engaged players from elsewhere: since the place itself was so small this is not surprising. This was the game during which the Turton goalkeeper made bets with the spectators around his posts, but he cannot have been too leisured because the ball was in Turton's half for sixty-five minutes of the ninety. Darwen were much improved and won by a single goal scored after twenty minutes: in a scrimmage three Darwen players each 'checkmated' a man and Marshall scored. Later, they claimed a second goal when the Turton goalkeeper carried the ball through, but the umpire was too far away to give it.

Earlier criticism, said the communicator in his report of this game, may have stirred up great local comment, but was purely for the good of the club, to point out the weak part of the play. 'We may be hard to please but we are far from satisfied with the passing and crossing', and the team will never be able to excel until they keep cool. Turton had more runners but, to emphasise the point, 'though running once upon a time could win a game it cannot now'.

There followed vignettes of some of the players that mixed praise with analysis. Duxbury was small but fearless. McWetherill had jocular good humour. There is no mention of his play, and during the next season he was to be replaced by the younger Tom Brindle. Marshall 'has become known by all the adjoining clubs', and in consequence heavily marked in recent matches. Robert Kirkham has 'commendable little tricks' but could be swifter so as not to be a drag on Marshall – evidence again of the two-man interpassing advance. James Knowles, at this time still a forward, is a 'little hot-headed, dash-at-it, neck-or-nowt, go-a-head player, and although he has not much to say, if he thinks he is being sat on by an opposing player he would as soon recommend him to a warm climate as anything else.' Tom Bury is a good header of the ball and an excellent passer, and W. Kirkham did 'dodging pranks and antics with the ball. He was a dancing master. Opponents stood off him sooner than look foolish.' Amid the chaos of the forward packs this must have been very difficult to achieve, and remarkable.

An approaching storm

Throughout March, while the communicator was analysing Darwen's football team, the Manchester cotton market declined. Asia was over-supplied. Both prices and the volume of business kept falling. Manufacturers saw their capital diminish week by week. In Blackburn there were two mill failures and in Darwen a joiner and builder went bankrupt for £2,600. The *Darwen News* reported that William Marsden, a 27-year-old quarryman who could not work because of illness, killed himself by jumping into a disused mine shaft.

For these uncertainties the announcement that Parliament would grant Darwen a Charter of Incorporation was ironic comfort. But the battle for independence had been won. Darwen would be separate from Blackburn, and become a borough in its own right. There would be Health Board elections at the end of March, and for the new municipality in May. These elections, it was expected, would be keenly and even bitterly contested. The formation of a local Conservative Association had caused what the *Darwen News* called 'a murky atmosphere', and divisions within and between families of the ruling elite.

'The Conservatives are willing for the sake of office to adopt Liberal principles,' complained a Liberal meeting convened by Eccles Shorrock, Jr, but as much to the local point was the fact that Shorrock's own life and relationship with his brothers was beginning to unravel. Shorrock's relatives said that he had misread the world market in which costs were rising and margins falling, and that he was to blame for their poor trading positions. They wanted to liquidate and restructure the companies to avoid catastrophe. Shorrock had the respect of his operatives because of his efforts during the Cotton Famine, and resented what he seems to have regarded as family interference.

That there had been attempts at compromises and expedients is indicated by a property auction at the end of January, when the Shorrocks tried to offload Entwistle Colliery but on the day withdrew it from the sale; or perhaps it did not reach its reserve, because by 1878 Darwen's coal pits were nearly exhausted. In the same sale Charles Costeker was the buyer, or at least the auction bidder, for the investment purchase for £810 of Spring Bank, the gentleman's residence rented by Josiah Singleton for his boarding school.

Shorrock's behaviour became more erratic, and his doctor persuaded him that for his health's sake he should travel abroad. Shorrock agreed, applied for a passport, and was gone soon after the auction. Maybe the personal nature of his troubles obscured from other people the fact that they were the lightning flickers of the approaching storm.

Local rates

Cotton spinning and weaving benefited unevenly from different phases of the trade cycle, and it is thought that, during the twenty years of poor trade after 1878, margins in spinning narrowed more than in weaving. Operative spinners themselves often contracted with the mill owner and employed their own piecers, whom they did not always want to join them in a union.

In the slumps of the late 1830s, and early 1840s, when the Hilton family went bust, disputes over spinning rates were bitter and it took unionism a long time to recover, just as it took a long time for the employers to see the benefits of collective bargaining. Workers often wanted local rates and direct local action, while union leaders were keener to get the confidence of all employers. Women and children often saw their work as temporary: their low wages restricted what they could pay in union subscriptions, which in turn reduced the ability of a union to offer accident insurance and sickness or unemployment pay.

This was the world in which, on Tuesday, 19 March 1878, as conditions worsened, the Employers' Association summoned the Operative Power Loom Weavers representatives to a meeting in Manchester, when they proposed a 5 per cent cut in piece-rates.

Blackburn weavers had won a good rate in 1852, but Oldham had not had an increase since 1834, and went on strike, saying that the reduction would be disastrous. In Darwen the employers, led by William T. Ashton, proposed a 10 per cent cut, and the union called a mass meeting to discuss its response. In Darwen 10,000 people would be affected by a cut or a strike, and while they held their breaths the football team beat Witton 1–0, a game that cast another light on tactics.

At the kick-off John Lewis sent the ball to the right wing and raced ahead with the other forwards, who had an advantage in front of the goal of five men to three. The ball was centred and there was a scrimmage, from which Darwen failed to score. Witton immediately altered their tactics and went on a defensive game: their backs and halves played in front of their own goal, leaving six men to chase Darwen's outfield ten. It became a pile-up in the Witton goalmouth, and at one point Darwen's backs were involved in a scrimmage there. Finally W. Kirkham dragged three or four defenders away and Darwen scored. In the second half they claimed another goal when Marshall chested the ball through but Witton appealed for offside; the referee agreed and threw the ball up to restart. Later he disallowed a third, but Darwen had displayed 'delightful passing like we have not seen since 1878 began'.

A few days later, on 25 March, William Snape, Chairman of the Local Health Board, arrived at

Darwen station bearing the actual Borough Charter. Fog signals were exploded on the line, and the bells of Holy Trinity Church rang out. Snape was escorted in triumph to the Free Library, where Charles Costeker read out the Charter, and made a rousing speech: 'We hug our Charter to our breast, and bid defiance to an insolent and jealous world . . .'

It was the realisation of the mill-owning elite's dream, but it came when the gap between their interests and those of their workers was about to be violently exposed.

Let's have a riot!

Darwen weavers wanted to negotiate short-time working instead of a reduction in piece-rates and for a moment there was indecision among the owners: makers of coarse to medium-quality cloths wanted reductions, finer spinners were willing to have short time, owners of smaller factories dithered. Then there was a second employers' meeting at the Mitre Hotel, Manchester, conveniently near the new Victoria Station. Colonel R. Raynsford Jackson of Blackburn was in the chair, and after forty minutes representatives of the Amalgamated Association of Operative Spinners, and of card room hands from Blackburn, Darwen and Accrington, were called into the room and told that the employers had come to a unanimous decision to enforce the 10 per cent cut. The unions tried to negotiate, but the masters said that if any strike occurred it would be met by a closure of all other mills.

The first mass meeting to discuss this was in Accrington. One delegate said that they should resist to the death, and blamed the Government for the bad state of trade. A voice from the back called out: 'Let's have a riot!'

On Wednesday, 17 April, the *Darwen News* ran a midweek Special Edition to report the meetings in

Darwen and Blackburn, both of which resolved upon a strike. Saturday's paper pleaded for conciliation. 'Men must either trust one another's candour or they must give up all hope of amicable debate.' These were probably the words of the editor John Wardley, who was a member of a devout Baptist sect, but they will have echoed the sentiments of the paper's owner and Chairman of the Health Board William Snape. Snape was sixty years old, the son of a jobbing builder, and because he could draw he had been apprenticed to a designer of patterns for carpets and wallpapers. He was the artistic half of a paper-staining business bought out by the Potters, which made him reasonably well-off and able to play local politics. He dabbled in other businesses, never brilliantly, was to sell the paper to J. J. Riley, and was kindly, generous and popular: an ideal figurehead, created by the boom years that were ending.

By the time his paper made its appeal thirty-four mills were stopped, including the Shorrock factories, the Exors of Nathaniel Walsh and W. T. Ashton's Hope Mill. Eighteen were on short time at the old rates, including John Walsh's Atlas. One or two mills were running three or four days a week at a 7.5 per cent cut. There were eleven spinners at Atlas Mill, who paid their own piecers. Money was being paid to all striking spinners who belonged to the union, and to three piecers who didn't.

Alongside this hard news the paper ran an article about 'Music of the Roman Empire', which discussed the Emperor Caligula's training in the arts; and it summarised the football season. Tom Hindle and John

Lewis had been to Manchester to see Birch entertain Queen's Park, and had 'not altogether wasted their time'. The Darwen first team had played against the reserves, who included a future star in the little half-back W. Moorhouse.

Statistics showed that in the 1877/8 season the team had played seventeen matches, won twelve, drawn three and lost two, with twenty-three goals for and seventeen against, five of which had been conceded at Partick. The reserves had played eleven, won ten and drawn one, and scored thirty goals with only two against.

As significant for the future was the announcement that there would be a benefit match to finance improvements to the ground: the slope was no doubt responsible for the poor drainage and mud, and would be levelled. And there was an extraordinary conclusion.

'We have searched the season's summaries of matches and are unable to find results equal to these in any of the London or provincial papers, and we venture to predict that if the team will only keep united and practise a little in the summer we shall possess a team quite equal to meet the Wanderers for the final heat in the Association Cup next season.'

Does not this prediction go beyond even the criticisms of the team? These had marked a transition from football as a social pastime to team-building for its own sake, and in pursuit of a standard. Is this new hopefulness not ambition, and maybe self-delusion, on a grander scale? It offers for a first recognisable time the hope of victory through quality that is the dream of spectator sport football: the proxy fulfilment that means so much in the lives of people who have so little; and in the months that followed many people in Darwen were to have little indeed, apart from what J. J. Riley was to call 'Football Mania'.

The benefit match to improve the ground duly took place on Easter Monday, when the Darwen first eleven were beaten 1–0 by Twenty Two Gentlemen of the Town, whoever they were, presumably out-of-condition shopkeepers and barmen; but receipts did not come near the £300 cost of the ground improvements, the residual debt from which was the real background to what followed.

When the cricket season opened, with the Temperance Association Brass Band to play in the intervals, it was mere forced jollity before a storm. The railway company said that compared to the previous Easter holiday 1,313½ fewer passengers had travelled from Darwen (was the child half a boy or a girl?) and shopkeepers began to complain about the fall in their business.

Then, after another mass meeting of two or three thousand, more workers came out on strike. The employers refused to budge, and what followed were the famous Darwen riots of May 1878.

Burnt in effigy

It was a week of lulls, intermittent bad weather, drunken yobbishness, occasional more embittered outbursts, and differing reactions from the authorities. On the first night a crowd seems to have been refused liquor by Richard Sharples, the licensee of the Bird in Hand beerhouse, at which they burned Sharples in effigy, smashed his windows, and went to the William T. Ashton mansion 'Ashdale' on the edge of the moors above the town.

Ashton was forty-two years old and his wife, Grace, of the Deakin family, thirty-four. They were to have nine children in all. Ashton was a forceful and contra-dictory character who later in life fought with passion for people to have free access to the moors, across which as a young man he had ridden to oversee Shorrock's coal pits. 'Under the wide summit,' he was to write, 'there is a tract of land unchanged in a land where everything else is changing . . . the ancient Britons of whom we know so little and have lost so much, found it as we see it now . . .' This from a man who was simultaneously a polluter, an implementer of sewage pipes and water works, a prime mover in the Mechanics' Institute, and ruthless in the Employers' Association. He was unpopular because when he addressed his workers he would talk about his own days as an operative, working twelve hours a day for a few shillings, none of which his audience denied. It was just that they knew how he had been promoted by his rich Shorrock relatives and was the first to slash wages. So they burned him and his wife in effigy, smashed their windows, and damaged their grounds.

Mrs Ashton was lucky to escape a stone that came through a window as she ran upstairs, but weavers loyal to the family smuggled the children out of the back and protected the front until the police arrived, wielding their staves as they dispersed the crowd. Later, police cutlasses were issued but never used. The crowd drifted into the town, where they broke more windows, including some in the police station. Then rain fell, which, said the *Darwen News*, 'had a tendency to render the streets quiet.' Glaziers went out at four in the morning to repair the pub, but it was some time before the damage to 'Ashdale' could be made good. Today it is an old people's home.

The next morning the soup kitchens of the Reverend Philip Graham's Relief Committee opened, and in the afternoon and evening people felt safe enough to go to the shops: but the following night there were more protesters on the streets, by which time more police had arrived, and charged to break them up.

At this point, on the morning of Friday, 11 May, the Bellman, appointed by the old manorial court and presumably self-important yet angered by the irrelevance of his office, called for a meeting on the moors. Speeches were made that criticised the roughness shown by the police, and there was some rowdyism. It was agreed to meet again at nine that night. At least 2,000 people gathered in Duckworth Street, at the bottom of Bolton Road. They carried sticks, poles, pokers, axes, hammers, hatchets and cow rakes, and a ringleader made a speech. 'Choose your man,' he said. 'Hit him. Leave others behind to trample him.' They then marched on the police station.

Captain Moorsom, Deputy Chief Constable of Lancashire, had arrived to oversee Superintendant Beyring, and they sent for the Reverend Graham and Charles Costeker, respectively Chairman and Clerk to the Magistrates. Graham and Costeker arrived and at once showed their mettle. They entered the crowd, spoke to the ringleaders, and asked them to disperse. The ringleaders agreed, provided that the police also withdrew when there was no actual disturbance. Graham and Costeker went inside to negotiate this but while they were doing so something happened in the crowd, violence started and showers of stones were thrown. Several policemen were injured, two of them badly.

At this Graham asked Moorsom to withdraw his men. Moorsom agreed, but some of them stayed on the street and arrested members of the crowd who were carrying poles.

Provoked, the crowd returned and threw more stones. Moorsom himself was hit, and taken to the Smalley's Arms with cuts to his cheekbone and eyebrow. Doctor Armitage was summoned and arrived with a colleague. The mob wandered around until midnight, some demanding money or liquor from public houses, but went away when more rain fell.

In the early hours, when all was quiet, the Chief Constable himself arrived. 'It has been remarked,' said the *Darwen News*, 'that water is a more effective method of preventing a disturbance than policemen.'

Next day the paper rushed out another Special Edition, which reported riots in Accrington, Padiham, Clitheroe, Preston, Oswaldtwistle and Burnley. Young people from Darwen had gone to join the riot in Blackburn, where the home of Colonel Jackson, Chairman of the Employers' Association, was burned down. In Great Harwood a magistrate, Mr Williams, had fired shots from his window and wounded several attackers.

In Darwen itself that Saturday there was a drenching thunderstorm. Thomas Wetherall of Queen Street Mill went bankrupt, and the Relief Committee dispensed 200 loaves and 1,400 quarts of soup. Christopher Shorrock of Moss Bridge Mill and the Walsh brothers offered relief to their own operatives who were in want.

The next day saw the first ever Sunday sitting of the Darwen magistrates. Various rioters, young women as well as men, all cotton operatives, were put up, and Graham and Costeker dismissed the first three cases 'to show that they did not wish to proceed to extremities'. In the afternoon troops passed through on their way to join the Dragoons who had been called to quell the riots in Blackburn: twenty-two men of the 17th Lancers and forty-five of the 54th Foot.

Joan O'Dicks will pay

On 12 June the Collection from Mills, Workshops and the General Public for the Relief of Necessitous Weavers, Winders, Warpers etc published its seventh set of accounts since the strike began. It had paid out some £160 with contributions from fifty-seven publicans and thirty workshops: printing, paper, and brick and tile works, quarries and masons. Its list of contributions from mills still working includes comments written in dialect or semi-literate spelling:

> Tilda Robottom (under no 2) ul pay
> When id feyther geds his penshun.

'No 2' , or Number Two, was an overlooker at Bank Top Mill. Against Deakin's Culvert Mill is the note:

> Joan O'Dicks will pay next week, if
> we'll relieve her brother, who is receiving
> pay from Spinners.

Spinners would be the official union; and against W. H. Gregson's mill is the note:

If Ralph Fish doesn't pay next week
we'll find him a wife to.

The voices of the common people, from that day
to this; but when both strike and lockout finished
at the end of June the workers went back defeated,
with a 10 per cent reduction. Yet they knew where
they stood, and somehow it is the masters who seem
alienated.

Even during the Cotton Famine, when the
Reverend Philip Graham chaired an earlier Relief
Committee, the town had stayed united, its little
individuality intact; and even the struggle between
the Ratepayers' Association and the elite had brought
improvements, acknowledged by all except perhaps
the unhappy Eccles Shorrock, Jr. Now there were
wounds of a kind not seen since the early days of
power looms. What riots, strikes and lockouts induced
in Darwen was a state of shock: the political paralysis
that the journalist J. J. Riley was to describe, and to
link to Football Mania.

James Huntington, the Potters' wallpaper partner,
was chairman of the Darwen Conservative Association
but early in June he unexpectedly died. The Reverend
Philip Graham was elected in his place. The first
municipal elections had been scheduled for May, but
because of the industrial troubles postponed until
the end of July, when a lively contest was expected.
It did not take place. There were to be three councillors for each of six wards, but the Conservatives
did not nominate a single candidate, and neither did
the Ratepayers' Association. Eighteen Liberals were

elected unopposed. Two thirds of them were former members of the Board of Health. The public showed extremely little interest, said the *Darwen News*, and the thing was done with neither trouble nor cost. At the first council meeting William Snape was elected both mayor and the town's first alderman.

Four months earlier there had been fog signals, church bells and rhetoric. Now, after so many years of hoping, there was a blank. It was an unusual situation, and it must have been brought about by discussions among the Conservatives themselves: Philip Graham, Charles Greenway, William Huntington. Graham's instinct must have been that the town did not need more disharmony. It is as though he and his colleagues had been made to realise that serious politics meant class war, and they turned away, and settled for as decent an administration as could be managed.

Charles Costeker, in private a staunch Conservative, was in public a seemingly unaligned conciliator, and was to make great play of his own and the football club's political neutrality. It must also have given him more power when decisions were more practical than partisan. James Walsh, on the other hand, had made it clear that he did not want to stand for election, even as a Liberal. He wanted less power, an early sign of the way in which an educated generation of the mill owner class began to drift away from its origins: men had seen wider horizons, and joint-stock finance was both safer and made their personal presence less important; and their wives could make homes in places where when the sheets were hung out to dry they were not speckled with soot from mill chimneys.

Whatever the mixture of reasons that lay behind it, to field no candidates was a remarkable decision, and the Conservatives repeated it at the next election.

Bowled by Moorhouse

Trade was as sluggish as local politics were moribund, but the weather must have been pleasant on the last Saturday in July, because 4,000 people attended the fifth Annual Sports Festival and Gala of the Cricket and Football Club. Sixty pounds were offered in prize money, less than the previous year because of the costs incurred in levelling the field. Tommy Marshall won the professional hundred-yards sprint in thirteen seconds, and played for Darwen's first team side that beat the reserves 2–1 in the five-a-side football knockout for a prize of £3.

At the beginning of September cricket and football overlapped by two or three weeks. Crookes, the cricket club professional who had also played in the football team, was leaving Darwen and appeared in two special matches. He played for Darwen Landlords versus Darwen Tradesmen, who included a professional from outside named Harwood, and his benefit match was a larger affair that drew £40 in gate money.

Crookes's Eleven, which was criticised in the paper on the grounds that it was not as strong as it might have been, played George Walsh's Eleven, which included the immortal A. N. Hornby, who earlier in the year had visited Australia with the England party. They played a single Test match, in Melbourne, where Hornby lived up to his reputation for being involved in bizarre incidents: on this occasion he jumped into the crowd to make a citizen's arrest of an unruly spectator. England lost, Hornby's batting failed, and he bowled his only spell in international cricket: seven maidens in which he took a wicket. Now, in Crookes's benefit match, he was bowled by Moorhouse for six.

Small, moustached, wiry and cheeky, Moorhouse was nineteen and had been born in Ashton. He was a loomer, lived with his mother and five siblings in Brook Street, Darwen, and was about to force his way into the football first eleven.

It is a romantic notion, but not an impossible one, that when Moorhouse bowled to Hornby, Jimmy Love and Fergus Suter were in the crowd and saw it happen.

Love and Suter

Forty years later the *Darwen News* obituary of Fergus Suter said that he arrived in the town some time in that September of 1878, and the corroboration is that he had no sooner arrived than he was asked to play for Turton in their Challenge Cup, which would have been a four-a-side knockout at their annual fair. Turton were runners-up, their prize money was £3, and Suter was given his share.

Apart from this there is little hard fact about the arrival in Darwen of either Love or Suter. At the time there was disinformation about professionals, and later there were merely journalistic anecdotes, so that different histories give different accounts. Perhaps the safest to believe is that of J. H. Catton, the journalist who also arrived in Lancashire in 1878 and wrote his memories of early professionalism some twenty years later. He said that, after a friendly in which he played for Partick, Love stayed in Darwen, and some time later Suter wrote to Tom Hindle saying that he proposed to move south and could he get a game? Some accounts say that Suter arrived with his brother, the Partick goalkeeper Edward, and an unnamed third party; others that the two Suters and Love arrived together. In the summer of 1878

Fergus was twenty, and it seems plausible that when he took such a big step in life his brother would have travelled with him to see that he was settled: there is no record of Edward staying in Lancashire.

Almost all this history is anecdotal, and it does not mention existing friendships made in Partick between Love, Suter and W. Kirkham, or suggestions made by Kirkham to the player-secretary, Tom Hindle, or conversations between Hindle and other committeemen such as Thomas Duxbury and George Walsh. But it is hard to believe that nothing of these sorts took place, or that nobody realised what Love and Suter could bring to the team: namely, Love's terrific dribbling and scoring power, and Suter's ability to visualise and control the tempo of a match.

What is definite about Suter is that earlier in the summer of 1878 he and his Partick chum Hugh McIntyre decided to advance their football careers with Glasgow Rangers, for whom both played in a trial match in August. Suter was in the Probables Eleven and McIntyre the Improbables, but it was McIntyre who was chosen for the first team and Suter who was not. It is this rejection that seems to have persuaded him to write to Hindle and try his luck in Darwen.

If this and his cool presence in early team photos tell us anything about him it is that he had a powerful sense of his own worth: he was a stonemason like his father and had the dignity of a craftsman, and a determination to control his life as far as he was able. He was the second of three brothers and their mother was thirteen years older than their father. The family moved house to be near areas of new construction, from Blythswood, where Fergus was born in 1857, to Merkland Street in Partick by the time of the 1871 Census, according to which they had two young men lodgers, and the household included a five-year-old girl named Hannah Lemon. Was she a grandchild from an earlier marriage that had widowed Mrs Suter?

Jimmy Love was older than Suter, already thirty-one and unmarried when he moved to Darwen, and had been born in Girvan on the Ayrshire coast. His tailor father had moved to Partick for work and their tenement block in Castlebank Street was in 1871 typical of the melting pot. Most of the people who lived there had been born outside Glasgow and seven were Irish. Jimmy had an older sister and three brothers and they were all in work, Jimmy and one of his brothers in the shipyards. But that was in 1871, when both the Love and Suter families, one feels, were well able to stay above disasters. What happened later we can only guess. For instance, did W. Kirkham lose his job in Partick, or was he on a contract, to install new machinery, say, that ended? Was Suter laid off? Was Love?

Love played for Partick in Darwen on New Year's Day 1878, but if that is when he stayed behind he is not shown as having appeared at once in the Darwen first team. Does that mean he played in the reserves? Again, some accounts say that when he did arrive he was found a job in a Huntington-run paper mill, and others that he worked in Walsh's Orchard Mill. Both are possible: perhaps he arrived when the cotton mills were shut or on part-time, and was given a temporary place in a paper works. Whatever happened, he was an incomer given a job when local people were being laid off, and because of this the influence of the Darwen committee is obvious. He was let in to play football.

There were several stonemason's yards in Darwen at the time, and doubtless Suter did work in one of them for a while. The story that he gave up because Darwen's yellow stone was harder to work than Glasgow's red may or may not be true. More to the point is that some time towards the end of 1878, and inspired by the sight of a cricket professional, he decided that it was as reasonable to work for a living at football as at anything else, and pointless to pretend otherwise.

People seem to have been too surprised by this honesty, and too much in need of his services, to deny him.

Catton wrote in 1900 that 'members of the club contributed a little each week to keep him in necessaries, as they had probably done for Love . . .' Chief among those members, one presumes, was George Walsh, the 27-year-old cashier of Orchard Mill and treasurer of the football club. Catton emphasised that Peter Andrews and James Lang, who were in Sheffield by 1877, and Archie Hunter, who joined Aston Villa in 1878, were Scots who moved to better jobs and then found football clubs. Suter, he insisted, was the first actual professional. Catton also said that Hugh McIntyre wrote to Tom Hindle; what became of this is not clear, except that McIntyre joined Blackburn Rovers in the spring of the following year.

Another but very different newcomer to the Darwen team was James Gledhill, a 23-year-old newly qualified doctor and surgeon born and practising in Manchester, although he was to move in the prime of his life to Chadderton, near Oldham, where he lived just around the corner from my maternal grandparents. Photos show a large, bearded, somewhat abstracted and eccentric figure; he played centre forward and according to the football annuals was 'a thorough hard worker who passes well and never tires'. Since it was said in a *Lancashire FA Annual* that he 'plays too much to the left side' one assumes he was left-footed. His centre-forward partner, Jimmy Love, was praised for his dribbling, and it may be that this was an early instance of a classic central striking combination: the big man who creates space and lays the ball off for his smaller and more skilful partner.

The facilities for obtaining drink

New arrivals promised lively events on the field, and in early autumn there were significant ones off it. Towards the end of the 1877/8 season Tom Hindle had suffered an injury that ended his playing career, but not his enthusiasm for the game, and he was still club secretary. He was also aware that by now there were numerous county football associations, all of whom ran cup competitions and played representative matches. In the first week in October he called a meeting in Darwen's Co-operative Hall at which Thomas Duxbury, the 32-year-old chairman of the club, proposed the motion that the local clubs should join together to form the Lancashire Football Association. At a subsequent meeting at the Volunteer Inn, Bromley Cross, Hindle was elected its secretary. He gave up his Darwen post and W. T. Walsh took over. They were all young together, and Hindle was involved in football administration until his death in 1927.

Darwen FC itself began the new season with victories against Manchester Wanderers, as the Birch club now called itself. The home game was won 5–1 and the away 6–2. Jimmy Love seems to have played in the first game, and James Gledhill made his debut in the second. They then won 4–1 against Edgworth, the nearby village team, and in the same week the *Darwen News* asked secretaries of local clubs to submit their reports on one side of the paper only, legibly written, and with the name and address of the sender.

At one public meeting, attended by only thirty people, it was proposed to ask the council to petition Parliament to bring Lower Darwen into the borough boundaries. John Gerald Potter, who had a factory in Lower Darwen and wanted to be sure what council rates he would pay, gave notice of his opposition. Eventually a deal was struck and the boundaries extended, but, without Conservative opposition on the council, rates rose to meet its ambitions.

Another meeting, over which the mayor, Alderman Snape, himself presided, formed a local branch of the British Women's Temperance Association. A speaker observed that 'drunkenness prevailed just in proportion to the facilities for obtaining drink'. Drink and gambling were the spectres that in respectable minds haunted sport, and it is worth remembering that, even in football-mad Darwen, the club was careful to convey the sobriety of all concerned, and to have an unimpeachable figure like the town clerk, Charles Costeker, as vice-president.

Sober or not, there must have been injuries among the actual players, because there were reserves in the side that could only draw 0–0 at Church, on the other side of Blackburn. They were reduced to ten men during the game and nearly beaten.

Grand football match by the electric light

Great excitement followed: the first floodlit game in Lancashire, at Darwen's Barley Bank. One of the features of early Sheffield football in the late 1860s had been the cup competitions run for their own profit by music hall proprietors, and the same entrepreneurial motive seems to have been behind the first floodlit match ever, at Bramall Lane in October 1878, which started a brief craze.

There was a match at the Oval a few weeks later, depicted in the *Illustrated London News*, and most games in that season's Glasgow Charity Cup were also under lights. The magnetos that powered the lights were driven by steam engines and the costs of fuel, carriage and labour were high. Games in the country towns were a complete failure, reported the Scots FA, but their overall net profit was £85, of which £50 was given to the still-open Unemployment Fund; another clue, perhaps, to explain why Love, Suter and McIntyre were keen to get out.

In Darwen the experiment took place at the end of October and yet interest was so great that most of the shops in the town centre closed early. It was advertised as a GRAND FOOTBALL MATCH BY THE ELECTRIC LIGHT and Darwen won 3–0 against a scratch

team from the Blackburn Association. Two electro-
magnetos from Orchard Mill were driven by two
steam engines: they produced 36,000 candle power.
The paper gave elaborate technical detail, far more
about the lights than the play, which was probably
not at full tilt, and the craze faded. It was too expensive to run. Eighty years later, in combination with air
travel, floodlit football helped to revolutionise European
club competition and the entire football scene.

Darwen's next game was more immediately serious:
Blackburn Rovers were beaten 1–0 at Alexandra
Meadows. Marshall and Love were the right-wing
pair and Gledhill 'showed to advantage' in the centre.
Darwen's crossing, and the passing of their halfbacks,
was praised. They scored a second goal but the umpires
did not agree and it was disallowed. Darwen agreed
to continue despite 'the ungentlemanly manners of
some Blackburn players'.

John Lewis had by now stopped playing for
Darwen. He had returned to Blackburn Rovers,
become club treasurer, and taken his ambitions with
him. The *Darwen News* criticism of the Blackburn
players is an early sign of what became over the next
few months a bitter rivalry: something modern in
feeling that involved incidents on the field, hypocrisies off it and the partisan wrath of spectators.

Darwen's regular fullback, McWetherill, must have
suffered fading form or a nagging injury because
for the next game against Sheffield Attercliffe the
seventeen-year-old Thomas Brindle replaced him.
McWetherill was older than most, born in Blackburn,
an overlooker with a wife and three daughters. Brindle

was described as a strong and powerful hard worker, with an accurate kick. The one criticism of him was that he stayed too near his own goal, but this may have been under orders, or the carefulness of someone who knew that he was inexperienced; and when the other fullback, Suter, roamed up behind the forwards he must have needed to know that there was steadiness behind him.

Brindle was born in Darwen and the photos show a tall, well-proportioned person with a strong, agreeable face, a level gaze and a moustache to make himself look older. Three years later he played for England but his career began with a stroke of bad luck. A Sheffield shot was beaten out by the goalkeeper, Booth, but it hit Brindle's leg and went in. Darwen equalised through a good move: Moorhouse to Love, to Gledhill, to Love again, who scored. Sheffield grew rough towards the end, it was reported, and it finished 1–1.

The score of the next match against a selection from the Blackburn Association is given as 7–0 in the following week's paper and 11–0 in J. J. Riley's later summary of the season's results. Love's dribbling was said to be prominent. Eleven-nil is repeated in later anecdotal accounts but it could well have been a misprint.

Although team sheets are not given in most of these match reports one must presume that Suter had established himself by now, and begun to influence the way the team played.

Got off at Entwistle

Darwen's next game, a 6–2 victory over Accrington, was not even covered by the paper ('pressed out', as the contemporary saying was) and then it was FA Cup time again. In the first regional round Darwen had a walkover, and in the second they drew their neighbours Eagley. A special train took Darwen supporters through the Sough Tunnel to Bromley Cross on the slopes above Bolton. Eagley's ground was five minutes' walk from the station and the players changed in the Volunteer inn, one of those pubs that loom large in early football history. Eagley were another working-class team. They played in white, and their goalkeeper-secretary was John Mangnall, the father of Ernest Mangnall, who in the early 1900s managed Manchester United: United's chairman at that time was J. J. Bentley, a journalist and later president of the Football League, who in 1878 was a teenager in his native Turton.

In winter, football would kick off early so as to finish in daylight, and since the mills stopped at half past twelve or one the tie would have started at two. The pitch sloped from end to end. It was frozen hard and there was a strong wind. Eagley won the toss, elected to play uphill and against the wind, and were under immediate pressure.

rgus Suter: the unabashed professional, as unfazed by the Blackburn photographer's bearskin as he was by privileged opponents and life in general.

Darwen in the late 19th century. Shorrock's India Mill and its chimney can be seen in the right foreground.

The cotton town riots in May 1878: the burning of Colonel Raynsford Jackson's house in Blackburn.

24 February 1872: the England versus Scotland game at Kennington Oval –
the chase breaks away from the scrimmage.

October 1878: the electric light match at the Oval. Note the umpire
with top hat and umbrella in front of the goal.

wen FC's first team photograph, taken in the spring of 1880 in front of the Alexandra
tel, formerly the Walsh family mansion, Orchard Bank. Back row from left: Duxbury,
1, Brindle, Broughton, Moorhouse. Middle row: Marshall, Rostron, Gledhill, Holden,
Kirkham, Bury. In front: Suter. Brindle and Marshall wear their England shirts.

The Wall Game
at Eton in the 19th
century. The ball is
locked in the scrimm

Eton boys in the 186

(*Above*) A.N. Hornby at Harrow.
(*Right*) Eton's Edgar Lubbock.

The Eton Cricket XI of 1876.
H.C. Goodhart is at the extreme right of the back row.

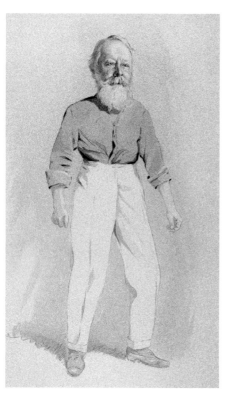

(*Above*) Sir Francis Marindin.

(*Left*) Arthur Kinnaird: an idealised tribute, published by *Vanity Fair*, 1889

(*Above*) Sir Charles 'J.C.' Clegg at the height of his powers.

(*Right*) Charles W. Alcock.

A comic legend surrounds this match, due to the fact that Dr Gledhill did not arrive until it had ended. He came from Manchester, and some accounts say that he got off the train at Bolton, two stops before Bromley Cross, and others that he got off at Entwistle, two stops after. At Entwistle he would have found himself among moorland sheep, at Bolton he would have walked around the town before discovering his mistake. Entwistle is funnier, but Bolton more likely.

Again, the *Darwen News* says that the team played with ten men throughout, but J. J. Riley's end-of-season summary reveals that another player travelling with the party went on for Gledhill but was then injured himself, so they were left with ten men anyway. Whichever it was, there were many struggles near the Eagley goal and Darwen scored a goal that was disputed and disallowed: someone headed in from a Suter free kick. In the second half Eagley had the wind, but Darwen showed fine passing and kept them on the defensive. The dodging of Love and W. Kirkham was singled out for praise, as were the fast runs of Tom Bury. Extra time does not seem to have been played. Both teams must have been exhausted by the conditions, and darkness was falling.

Away from the football pitch times were harsh. Despite reports of a colourful episode where a gorilla travelling to Bridgnorth in Shropshire escaped from its menagerie, the local news was torrid. In the severe frost many horses fell in the roadway, and a woman broke her leg in Hannah Street. An out-of-work man with a wife and three children attempted to kill himself by taking a threepenny rat powder.

The uplifting news concerned the football team. After the Lancashire County FA held its trial match at Barley Bank the committee voted for its team to play the Welsh FA at Chester, and Booth, McWetherill, Suter, Moorhouse, Bury and Gledhill all received a maximum five votes each, and four of them were to play in the match; which as it turned out came two days after Darwen's first game against Old Etonians, a clash of interests that did not help Darwen at all.

The men who did not play for the county were the goalkeeper, Booth, and fullback McWetherill, and they were either injured in the Eagley replay or judged to have played badly in the annual New Year's Day friendly against Partick, because they were not picked for Darwen's London games, and never recovered their first team status.

In the 21 December Cup replay Eagley were decisively defeated. Darwen were unchanged, Dr Gledhill arrived on time, and although the conditions were again bad they were 3–0 up at half-time and eventually won 4–1. Jimmy Love scored a hat-trick and Gledhill the other: a triumph, one assumes, for playing the ball wide and timely crossing. Then in the third round they were drawn to play Remnants at Kennington Oval.

Gaslight on cobbles; carol singers; mince pies in the vestry; snow blowing and not much actual cheer. Could it be true, the breezy prediction that this time they had a team good enough to challenge Wanderers in the final tie?

A lifted free kick

In the euphoria of their Cup victory and the knowledge that they were about to be the first Lancashire
team to play in London, the Darwen players may
have celebrated Christmas and the New Year not
wisely but too well, because in their customary 1
January fixture against Partick they were beaten 7–1.
At a time when Scots teams were losing their advantage this was a drubbing. The Lancashire papers said
that Darwen hit the woodwork several times, but the
Scottish FA Handbook reported that although Suter,
Moorhouse, Gledhill and Bury worked hard they
were out of luck, and were beaten by 'a capital passing
game'. McWetherill and Hayes were in the Darwen
team but did not play much thereafter. Maybe the
game was under the Scots offside and throw-in rules,
because two days later Partick beat Blackburn Rovers
4–2 'under English rules' in a much tougher encounter.

By then the frost that was to grip England for two
months had set in. Racing and steeple-chasing were
impossible and in the north building and outdoor
trades were laid off. There were strikes on the
Liverpool docks. The *Darwen News* lamented the
poor state of the cotton trade; local manufacturers
wanted to cut wages again and some mills were on

short time. The football team was the one thing the town could be cheerful about, but on 7 January, a Tuesday, they lost again, 2–1 in their return match at Sheffield Attercliffe. Snow lay on the ground and fell during the game. Suter played excellently despite being described as 'far from well'.

On 11 January their Lancashire Cup tie against Blackburn Rovers was frost-bound, but in midweek they recovered their form and beat Bolton Wanderers 8–0 on a hard and slippery pitch. In 1879 a goal could not be scored direct from a free kick, and reports of the match describe a ploy whereby Suter lifted a free kick into the air and Gledhill headed home: from the tone this was very unusual, and perhaps an invention.

Whether the cotton mill players were laid off, on short time, or recompensed for time spent playing or training is never discussed, but since there were midweek games as well as at the weekend, we might assume that mill owners were at the very least compliant, and did not dock men's wages.

By mid-January the campaign to finance the trip to London was in full swing. It began with an appeal in the *Darwen News* of 11 January to the effect that the club must raise money or give Remnants a walkover. 'Time was when we had eleven gentlemen players . . .' it said, but now the mill lads needed help. It was proposed to open a Public Subscription Fund. As it unfolded it became a brilliant spin-doctored campaign at a time when the town was riven and sullen, and confidence between masters and men at a low ebb, and an interesting light is cast on it by items in Darwen Public Library's Singleton Collection.

The tuck box in the attic

Josiah Singleton was born in Yorkshire in 1811 and went to Darwen as a schoolteacher. By the 1870s he ran his academy in the mansion 'Spring Bank', which he leased for £50 per annum plus a ground rent. His eldest son, Thomas, variously described as a machinist and a brass founder, was born in 1831 and had three sons of his own. Fletcher was born in 1857, Robert in 1859 and young George in 1867. There was a daughter older than George. Fletcher and Robert played for their Central Wesleyan Methodist Church football team, and in 1879 were among the twenty founder members of Darwen Rangers FC, a recreational club of aspirant young professionals: yarn agents, an auctioneer, the manager of Rochdale tramways.

Twelve years old, George was bright, and had been sent away to a better school. Robert's letters to him included the local football papers, details of Darwen Rangers, the Sunday School, and other documents of interest. George became a solicitor, and after his death sixty years later what is now called the Singleton Collection was found in his old school tuck box in the attic of his Blackburn law office.

The most interesting football material is J. J. Riley's local sports papers, which he seems to have published for a short time only in 1879. Riley, a shortish, strong-jawed character, was born in 1851 near Leeds and sent to grammar school. Then his father died, and at the age of nine Riley moved to Darwen with his sister and widowed mother. He was an errand boy, attended night classes at the Mechanics' Institute, and was apprenticed to a druggist, postmaster and printer named Gregson. In 1871 Gregson retired and Riley set up on his own. By 1879 he had bought a freehold, published his annual *Household Almanacks*, tried and failed to buy the *Darwen News* (he soon succeeded), and was the town's chief jobbing printer.

The Darwen Cricket and Football Times, which he soon changed to *The East Lancashire Cricket and Football Times*, and sold through seven newsagents across the area from Bolton to Accrington and Blackburn, was his first newspaper foray and both reflected and helped to create the town's football boom. It is full of trenchant and deliberately provocative writing, presumably by Riley himself, because he was already known as a forthright contributor to debates at the Literary Society. About the paper itself he wrote in a February edition of his hopes that 'a weekly journal of this description might be self-supporting', and a month later that the 'Darwen Committee solicited the formation of this new enterprise', but now that the publisher is losing money 'the Darwen Committee will not help and the publication will cease to live'.

At the end of the season Riley said that when the committee entered the FA Cup 'they had not the remotest idea of the gigantic proportions it would assume', and he seems to have had a point. In their excitement and unfamiliarity the committee appear to have turned this way and that, and to have whipped up people's hopes, not least those of Riley himself. His little sports paper seems ultimately to have failed: the money-raising benefit concert for which he printed and posted the bills did not.

The benefit concert

A concert to top up the Subscription Fund was announced in the *Darwen News* of 18 January, when the paper carried other stories headed DESPERATE STRUGGLE WITH A BURGLAR and SUSPICIOUS DEATH OF A LUNATIC PATIENT, and it took place in the Co-operative Hall on Monday, 27 January. It was organised by the club chairman, Thomas Duxbury. Charles Costeker, as town clerk and vice-president of the club, was in the chair and seems to have sat on the platform with the players and the piano which was part of the £2 4s. 0d. hire of the hall.

Costeker's opening speech gives a good idea of his style, and of the town's uneasy calm. He began by associating the spirit of the team with the honest nature of the place itself:

> We play an uphill game gamely. If we can we win. If we lose we say nothing about it. We believe that football, cricket and other such athletic games have a tendency to improve the moral as well as the physical condition of our young men, and we think that the people of Darwen should support a town's club of this description.

I understand that the Committee in selecting a chairman have looked out for one whose political colour is not an extreme one, and I believe that they have succeeded in this respect, as I believe that no man in Darwen has less feeling in political matters than myself . . .

Not bad, with the professionals behind him on the platform, and in the press seats the *Darwen Times* man poised to make snide comments about the hall itself, the pride and joy of the Co-operative Movement. It was built to hold 1,300 but its heating is uneven, said the paper, starving cold on stage and at the front, stifling at the rear. The stairs at the head of the ante-room should be draught-proofed, and the reserved seats given cushions. If you're sitting at the front take a railway rug.

Draughts, and the time it must have taken to get people on and off the platform notwithstanding, the programme began with the 2nd Lancashire Regiment of Volunteers' Band playing the overture 'Jean de Paris', which was followed by a scratch team of ladies and gentlemen from the Darwen Musical Union singing glees. When the Union was founded in 1877 it featured numerous members of the mill-owning families as performers as well as sponsors, but on this occasion the soprano, Mrs W. S. Ashton, was absent with a cold. Whether this was tactical or not is unclear, but in general the local political leaders, who were also the town's richest men, did not contribute to the fund and do not seem to have attended the concert. Is the subtext of Costeker's speech that these people did not want to be seen together, not even in support of the football club? If it is, the feeling between them must have been sullen indeed.

Mrs Ashton's place as a soloist was taken by Miss King, the daughter of a toyshop owner, who was at least accompanied on the piano by Miss Huntington: the Huntingtons, a family part Liberal and part Tory, were the incoming partners of the Potters in their paper-staining factory. One of them had trained in industrial design in Paris.

Tommy Clapham came next. He was twenty-seven years old and had been born blind, but musically gifted, in the hillside village of Pickup. He played his concertina and was at that time the licensee of a beerhouse called the Spinners Arms in Bolton Road. He was a local character who played at all sorts of events for sixty years, concertina and fiddle, just as the town's working-class dialect poet 'Shakespeare' Eccles wrote verses to order for weddings, funerals and even the opening of new mills. When Tommy Clapham was old, and spent most of his time in the Reform Club, he told the *Darwen News* that 'music is good for people and makes them happy and anybody who doesn't like music has something wrong with them'. He had been married in the Railway Road Wesleyan Church, which today houses a cut-price supermarket.

Tommy was followed by Thomas Livesey, a rentier member of the mill-owning family, who was said to possess a 'pure tenore' voice, and after him Messrs. Hindle, father and son, played a cornet duet, and the local shopkeeper James Halliwell sang a comic song entitled 'Johnny Morgan'. Mr W. H. Black, an accountant and the auditor of the Subscription Fund, gave two readings in Lancashire dialect and Joseph Hall, another accountant, a speech from what was described as 'the lobby scene' in *Hamlet*. O, what a rogue and peasant slave am I? Maybe. The wine and spirit merchant Mr Goodall's euphonium was accompanied by the schoolmaster Mr Wilmore's piano.

Many years later George Butterworth, who conducted the Musical Union glees, and as a boy had sung in a choir at the India Mill Art Treasures Exhibition, recalled that his regular vocal quartet had blacked up for the benefit concert and styled themselves the Zulu Minstrels: Butterworth himself, James Livesey and his brother Ralph, who sang alto, and Ashworth Higham. They were young dashers, as it were, and thought it a bit daring.

The benefit concert was a one-night music hall that would not shock the ladies. There were no jugglers, dancers, smutty comedians, contortionists or dog acts, and presumably no prostitutes on the prowl, as there might have been in an actual music hall. But there was a respectable consensus, and its significance was that only for the football team would the likes of the moneyed Miss Huntington and blind Tommy Clapham appear on the same non-religious stage. The concert was a triumph of the aspirant shop-keepers and lower-level professionals, whereas the Subscription Fund expressed the feelings of the less important.

Thomas Duxbury was secretary of the Fund, H. Coulthurst, who ran an iron foundry, treasurer, and the accountant W. H. Black the auditor. Money came in over several weeks and the accounts were finalised in April, when it was shown that the concert cleared £45 15s. 0d. and the subscriptions £107 14s. 4d. Of what we might call members of the elite the Huntington brothers gave £21 2s. 1d. between them, James Christopher Ashton a guinea, George Walsh a pound and the Mayor, Alderman Snape, ten shillings. Over seventy mills and workshops took collections, and most pubs, alehouses and butchers' shops. The Misses Mary and Sarah Sutcliffe, who ran a confectioner's in Bridge Street, gave five shillings, and literally hundreds of individuals gave pennies and tuppences.

In the middle of this excitement the *Darwen News* published the club's accounts for the season 1877/8, which showed that it owed £219 18s. 4d. because of what it had cost to level and improve the Barley Bank ground. Gate receipts had been £202 1s. 7d., receipts from the Electric Light Match £46 17s. 10d. and from the annual sports £37 15s. 1½d. Refreshments and grazing (sheep to keep the grass down) raised £31 5s. 0d. It is perfectly clear, said the paper, that with equal receipts and no increase of expenditure the balance will be wiped away in 1879. In fact they were hit by the dream of success and never recovered from it.

Cushions and warming pans

Even in the 1950s, when I was a travelling reporter with Matt Busby's Manchester United, it took as long to get from Manchester to London as it would take us today to reach New York, and players who were stars then and have since become legendary always regarded it as a bit of an adventurous trip. Such journeys are as much in the mind as overland, and the emotions of the Darwen players who went to London on 29 January 1879 can only be imagined. They had travelled before to Glasgow and Sheffield, but this was different. This was momentous. It was historic, and they knew it, and so did the crowd who gathered at the railway station to see them off on the 2.30 p.m. to Manchester Victoria.

There were twenty-one in the party, but beyond the team and their umpire, Tom Hindle, none of them are named in the account of the journey written for the *Darwen News*. Only twelve persons seem to have been paid for by the club. So who were the others? Let us guess that Lucy Kirkham with her baby, Nellie, in her arms was one of the two unnamed women, and that J. J. Riley, who wrote an evident eyewitness match report in his paper, and James Christopher Ashton, the possible contributor of the

Darwen News colour piece, were among the men.
No doubt there was an extra committeeman or two,
and maybe a Walsh brother. The rest seem to have
been friends or relatives who went for the hell of it,
and why not?

Manchester Victoria was newly rebuilt, and imposed
upon the mess of medieval houses that had lined
the River Irwell and its little tributary the Irk,
so the first part of the group's walk across the city
centre to London Road (now Piccadilly) Station was
insalubrious. The Tramp Ward was nearby, where
homeless men and women lined up to spend the night
on a plank bed with a wooden pillow, and there was
an old mill housing cotton-waste dealers. There were
small workshops in yards, a boarding house, an under-
taker's, a fustian cutter in a cellar, a confectioner and
a beerhouse.

The old butchers' Shambles was still off the bottom
of Market Street, which was busy with trams and
people, shops and commercial hotels: the Albion, on
the left as they walked up, was where eight years
later the meeting to propose a breakaway British
Football Association would be held. The old eight-
eenth-century Infirmary still stood in Piccadilly itself,
and cotton goods warehouses, and the Queen's Hotel,
where eighty years later the Busby Babes would
sometimes have lunch on match days.

London Road Station was up the ramp that still
stands, and had a neo-classical facade and a gloomy
booking hall, with offices on its balconied landings,
like a provincial version of the old Euston. The team
would have each carried their luggage, and Lucy

Kirkham her baby, and when they got in the 4.50 Manchester, Sheffield and Lincolnshire train for St Pancras they thought it an improvement upon the third class carriages of the Lancashire and Yorkshire. There were cushions, warming pans and space for the luggage.

They arrived at St Pancras at 10.20 and went by the Underground to Aldersgate Street, where they had a thirty-five-minute wait for their connection to St Paul's. The mill lads joked, because they were both nervous and showing off, and the *Darwen News* colour piece conveys how provincial they were, and different to the other people on the platform. Was it written by the mill owner James Christopher Ashton? Probably, one feels, because of the way in which it is almost patronising but not quite. For example, did the waitress really believe that someone was French? Or was she a pretty girl, and a player flirted with her, and codded her along, as footballers have been known to do?

Whatever, at 11.30, nine hours after leaving Darwen, they arrived at Watson's Private Hotel, which faced the entrance to St Paul's Cathedral. They slept badly, and, like thousands of away teams since, had a bit of a morning wander and assembled at noon.

The Oval

In 1845 the Montpellier Cricket Club leased four acres of market garden and turfed them to make the Oval Ground in Kennington. They almost lost it to speculative builders in 1851, before Prince Albert intervened, and again in 1854, but good tenure was secured and the Montpellier Club metamorphosed into Surrey County Cricket Club. In 1858 there were 250 members and a pavilion was erected: it was neo-classical in style, with raked open seating on the roof, and stood next to the Surrey Tavern, which at the back had balconies and access to the field. Gasometers rose at the north-east corner, and football came to be played across the northern half of the outfield, with one goal in front of the gasometers. The marked-out pitch was surrounded by a rope. There was the beginning of turf banks around the main perimeter, and benches in summer, when potboys from the Tavern would stroll round crying, 'Orders, gentlemen, orders!', and return with the drinks. A small flock of sheep was penned in one corner but it was hard to keep thistles down in the outfield because when the sheep were released to do their job they would rush to the more tender grass of the square. They were used to crowds because as well as cricket and football the Oval hosted rugby, cycling and baseball.

This range of events brought much-needed revenue to Surrey, who had bad seasons in 1878 and 1879: their best amateurs were either ill or unavailable because their businesses needed them, given the poor state of the economy. Since the Oval was a properly enclosed arena which could not be entered without payment, although people in surrounding houses looked on as they do today, the Football Association welcomed the receipts and stipulated that from the quarter-finals onwards all Cup ties must be played there. They were forced to review this by what happened to Darwen.

Before the Remnants game the Darwen players gathered at the Surrey Tavern, where presumably the teams changed, although this is not clear. It was very casual, said the *Darwen News*, and the Remnants men drifted in one by one. Everyone was on their best behaviour no doubt, and determined not to say the wrong thing: Remnants trying not to condescend, and Darwen not to look gauche. Yet as men shook hands and eyed one another, is it not possible that, through the Walshes and their sporting friends like A. N. Hornby, Darwen knew more about Remnants than Remnants did about Darwen?

Remnants

In the world of Gentlemen Amateur football there were many nuances. Some clubs were of a higher social class than others, and this applied in the provinces as well as around London. In 1879 Blackburn Rovers were seen as a gentleman's club, and Blackburn Olympic's millhands were more popular among ordinary spectators. In the Home Counties some clubs were also exclusive in terms of their level of play: if you weren't good you wouldn't get a game. Wanderers in their heyday, Old Carthusians and Old Etonians when they were active fell into this category. Royal Engineers were serious and military, Clapham Rovers serious but more middle class. A club like Remnants, based in Slough and playing on the Aldin House Preparatory School ground, was for upper-class people who knew one another, but weren't perhaps quite good enough to play for the finest teams.

Remnants were primarily a soccer club, but they would play other rules to get a fixture, and sometimes top players did turn out for them: the Old Etonian international de Paravicini was one and the Old Harrovian and Wanderers player Reginald de Courtenay Welch another. At the Oval they fielded a future international forward in E. M Hawtrey. Their recent record had been average. In 1878 they lost to Marlow in the semi-final of the Bucks and Berks Association Cup, and to Upton Park in the third round of the FA Cup. They played socially equal teams in Old Etonians and Oxford University but were beaten 4–0 by both. In the Cup they had just had a walkover in the first round and beaten Pilgrims 6–2 in the second. Perhaps the greatest hurdle that Darwen had to overcome was psychological: that of actually playing against a team of their social superiors.

Long trousers cut down

Throughout that Thursday morning there had been drizzle, which by the time the teams came out had turned to sleet, so that the hard ground had a thin coating of snow and the ball would run fast but erratically. The crowd was small and the press were in their places beneath the gasometers, although as they did in those early days they probably walked around and even chatted to the goalkeepers when play was at the other end. The first telephone to be used to report on a football match was one that J. H. Catton had nailed to a tree at Derby racecourse in the mid-1880s, although telegrams would be sent. During the Remnants game the editor of the *Sporting Life* in Manchester seems to have received telegrams when goals were scored and at half-time, and then sent them himself to the *Darwen News*, where a crowd had gathered in and around the office.

The east–west orientation of the Oval pitch often played a big part in football matches because of the strength of the east wind. The same original layout of the cricket pitch could also be a handicap, because the sun was always in a batsman's eyes. This Thursday the wind was strong, and unpleasant for the spectators, who must have been disconcerted by Darwen's raggedy appearance; it left no doubt that there were two worlds on the field. When good-quality football jerseys cost 5s. 6d., stockings half a crown a pair, flannel shirts 7s. 6d., caps a shilling, second-quality knickerbockers 6s. 6d. and the best shinguards five shillings, Darwen could not afford to be properly dressed. Tommy Marshall's actual mill wage, remember, was less than a pound a week. Although the forward Tom Bury always played in very light, thin shoes which gave him the touch to screw the ball in with his left foot in a style praised by Alcock's *Football Annual*, the team as a whole wore cast-offs. One or two wore braces over a dark shirt and most of those with knickerbockers had long trousers cut down, and there were all sorts of shirts. Two men wore sweaters. The journalist and football administrator N. L. Jackson called them, somewhat sneeringly, the 'Brummels' of the team, after the dandy 'Beau' Brummel, who had been a friend of the Prince Regent. The amazing Dr Gledhill could probably have afforded better gear than his colleagues but chose not to embarrass them.

The most blackguard thing

The referee who called the captains to toss for ends was Charles W. Alcock himself, the person whose ideas and generosity of spirit most influenced early football. When he left Harrow, Alcock had founded Forest and Wanderers, for whom he played with gusto. He supplemented his private money by working as a sports journalist. At first he left football administration to his older brother, J. F. Alcock, who at the meetings which founded the Football Association had proposed the motions to ban hacking and body-tackling. Later J. F. Alcock became involved with a woman who was probably a prostitute, married her, and in an unsavoury court case had her declared insane. He felt unable to continue a public life. Charles took his place on the FA committee and in 1869 became hon. secretary.

His impact was immediate. He knew that, to develop, football needed meaningful competition, and he inaugurated the international matches with Scotland and in 1872 the FA Cup. He was also a diplomat: he suggested that the Sheffield Association should join the FA but keep its own rules, confident that in time the majority idea would prevail. Alcock was also Secretary of the Surrey County Cricket

Club, which is why big football matches came to be played there. Although Alcock was paid by Surrey, the early Football Association was a voluntary organisation run on a shoestring by personally affluent men. It had no salaried office clerk until 1883, and Alcock himself was not paid until 1886. He was nevertheless Britain's first career sports bureaucrat.

As a player, Alcock won an England cap in 1875. He was six feet tall and a formidable runner, who in his prime weighed fourteen stone. 'The way Alcock used to knock a fellow over when he was trying to pace him I shall never forget,' said W. G. Grace, the England cricket legend who played soccer for Wanderers. For Alcock's part he said that the way his team-mate Grace once shoved him aside to score the goal himself was 'the most blackguard thing that ever happened to me during a long sporting career'. But there's the great Doctor for you. Alcock himself stopped playing in 1875, and in 1879 he was thirty-seven years old.

Duxbury floored

Knowles won the toss for Darwen and chose to play with the wind, but when the game kicked off a couple of minutes later it was Remnants who launched furious rushes. Suter showed great speed and judgement in stopping them, and clearing with either foot. Darwen slowly took control and most of the play was in the Remnants' half, until on the half-hour they broke away. Darwen's new goalkeeper, John Duxbury, moved from fullback, went for the ball but was charged over by the Remnant halfback Flower before he could reach it, and the right-wing forward E. M. Hawtrey nipped in to score. This inspired energetic Remnants attacks which Darwen again repelled, and in the last minute of the half Bury equalised with a header.

Remnants had the wind in the second half and went ahead almost at once through Dear. Against the wind and sleet, keeping the ball low and using their passing game, Darwen carried the game to their opponents and with a few minutes left Gledhill, described by J. J. Riley as 'a real trump', put W. Kirkham in to equalise. The gentlemen were tiring and desperate, and in their final flurry Darwen's right back, Brindle, kicked clear when he was surrounded by a pack of five Remnant forwards, and Duxbury made a crucial last-minute save.

There was now a lengthy consultation between the captains. Extra time was not mandatory but had to be mutually agreed: it had been played before, even in a Cup Final. Knowles was a man of few but decisive words and seems to have wanted to play again the next day. Remnants could not have guaranteed to keep their team together and wanted to play on. Perhaps Knowles sensed how tired they were, and he agreed to thirty minutes.

Almost at once Jimmy Love put Darwen 3–2 up with a shot that ricocheted in off the defender French and it was obvious that Remnants were spent. With lights coming on in the surrounding buildings, sleet still falling and the ball hard to see, Darwen did not defend, but took the game forward to the end.

The *Athletic News* said that Darwen were 'a good working team, rather light but fast forward, and all passing wonderfully'. Smart judges like N. L. Jackson emphasised later how they had been struck by Suter's quality, and how splendid his play was. For enthusiasts everywhere it was a giant-killing headline sensation, the first in the FA Cup. And a fluke, surely, which most of them thought could not be repeated. How could it be, when in the quarter-final, which would again be played at Kennington Oval, Darwen were drawn against the very Empire's lords and masters, Old Etonians?

PART TWO

Old Etonians

Wake up and reorganise

Old Etonians were the essence of Gentlemen Amateur football, and not least because their existence as a club was erratic. A group of Old Etonians formed a club at Cambridge in the 1840s, when they and some Old Salopians posted the first rules. Later the first university match was between Oxford and Cambridge Etonians under Field Game rules. A club to play soccer was formed in 1864, but compared to the old boys' cricket club, Eton Ramblers, it did not have a flourishing life. For the first two years of the FA Cup, for instance, Old Etonians did not enter, and in 1874 they entered but scratched from the first round. In 1875 and 1876 they entered and were beaten finalists, in each case after replays for which injuries forced them to make changes. In 1877 they again scratched from the first round, and fell into such abeyance that in 1878 they did not even enter.

This failure prompted an anonymous letter to *The Field*, in August 1878, which pointed out that the Ramblers made every member of the College cricket eleven a member, and invited others, so why could football not do the same, wake up and reorganise? Etonians responded to this, and the club was re-formed at a meeting in the Freemasons Tavern in

October 1878, when it was announced that they had already entered the FA Cup. Three legends of Gentlemen Amateur football were elected to the committee: the Hon. Arthur Kinnaird (later Lord Kinnaird), probably the best all-round player of his day, Francis Marindin and the Hon. Alfred Lyttelton, a flying right-winger of strong opinions. There were representatives of Oxford, Cambridge and the school, and the recent school leaver R. D. Anderson was made secretary. The cap was to be blue and white, the shirt to have an Eton blue body with white sleeves. Alcock's 1879 *Football Annual* said that there were sixty members. In his annual summary M. B. Hawke, the Keeper of the Field for 1878/9, was to welcome the foundation of the club, but his warmth represented a relatively new attitude.

When they woke up, and were able to pick their best eleven, Old Etonians were as good as anyone, and probably the most fearsome exponents of the old-style dribble and back-up game. That they woke up so inter-mittently, until it was more or less too late, is because men formed loyalties to other clubs, and because the dream of the Field Game was seductive, and its mythology potent. They may well have prevented wholehearted commitment to a soccer-playing club. After all, men who wanted to play soccer had numerous clubs they could join and turn out for as their leisure permitted. Kinnaird reckoned that he kept fit by playing four or five times a week, even after 1877, when he was made a partner in the merchant bank Ransom and Co. The Field Books show that in the 1870s he returned to Eton with the Gitanos, Wanderers and Old Etonians.

Gitanos, as their gypsy name indicates, were a lesser version of Wanderers. Both were clubs with no ground of their own, who went where fixtures presented themselves. The star Old Etonian forward H. C. Goodhart returned with both Gitanos and the Berkshire club Runnymede, and various lesser Etonians played for Remnants. Some of these games were under Field Game rules, and some Association. The classic club membership dilemma was that of Francis Marindin, when Royal Engineers met Old Etonians in the 1875 Cup Final. He played for both, and decided that the honourable thing to do was to turn out for neither.

There was also a contributory aspect in Eton educations. Etonians were encouraged in an attractive and sophisticated quality: the acceptance of human motives and frailties. The other side of this was, and perhaps still is, that they expected their own selfishness to be understood in the same way, and had no compunctions about it. If it was easier and as amusing to play for Wanderers, why not do so? If it was easier to scratch from the FA Cup than to chase up men to play, why not scratch?

Then at the end of the 1870s, in an instinctive response to the moment, to play became important: a definition, almost, of identity.

Floreat Etona

Even in the eighteenth century, Eton and Harrow looked the same from a distance, but up close were very different. Eton was richly endowed from the start, and Harrow was not. Eton catered for old money, and Harrow for new. Eton had the College with its Provost, Fellows and Collegers, and a school with a headmaster, and Oppidans living in boarding houses in the town and paying their way. As at Harrow, there were many extras and boys with private tutors, and the usual floggings, classical curriculum, fights with locals, and eccentrics.

Victorian change began at Eton in 1840 with the appointment of Provost Hodgson and Hawtrey as headmaster: nine generations of the Hawtrey family went to Eton, and one of them founded Remnants. Hodgson raised money to improve conditions for the Collegers and this affected Eton generally. Buildings were acquired, pulled down and rebuilt as new boarding houses. A sanatorium was erected. The disciplinary system placed trust in the boys and games were encouraged: cricket, racquets, fives, athletics, two kinds of football, rowing.

The river was in bounds but the road to it was not, a classic Eton contradiction like that by which roll-calls are called 'Absences'. Eton slang may not have passed into the wider English like 'footer', but was none the less vivid. 'Can you sock me the construe?' meant can you give me (as often as not for cash) the crib of a Latin or Greek translation. 'Sock' in another context meant to eat, probably greedily. A 'scug' was a boy who had no sports colours. A 'scug cap' was what he wore. A 'bury' was a bureau, the top half of which would be taken off and used as a book-case. 'Scug' is interesting: a nineteenth-century word for a new nineteenth-century notion, a snobbery whereby ability at sport conferred upon people a higher moral and social status.

Eton catered for old money, but in the 1840s a lot of old money was not in fact very old. Arthur Kinnaird may have been able to trace his landed power in Scotland to the Middle Ages, but much of the British peerage was new. In 1776 there were 199 peers, but by 1830 there were 358: new moneyed people who bought land, courtiers, military men who did well in the wars, coal owners, Indian nabobs. Irish and Scots peers were given seats in the Lords in return for political loyalty; and behind all these were the merchants and the professional and manufacturing people whose money was created by England's economic and colonial growth. Debates about the public schools were about how this enlarged ruling class should be educated, and in the end new privilege got what it wanted: instant traditions and an ideology that justified superiority and ambitions.

At Eton the fulfilment of this need was more subtle and ambiguous than at Harrow and other schools, but it took place none the less, and sporting myths were a similarly essential part of it. But because Eton always reckoned, perhaps, to turn out a bit more than just an English gentleman, its myths were insouciant and elegiac.

Chitty's eleven

At first the Eton romances were woven around cricket and boats. The defeat of 1845, when Westminster rowed an outrigger, was much mourned, and only partly assuaged by the river heroics of the oarsmen Bagshawe and Welby, and the famous Chitty's Eleven of 1847, when Harrow, Winchester and Westminster were all beaten at cricket. J. W. Chitty himself was Keeper of the Field, Captain of Cricket, and wicketkeeper. He had a splendid physique, but a youthful fever destroyed every hair on his body, eyebrows and lashes included. 'To play football in a wig was not easy,' records a memoir, but he did it, and his sang-froid on the way to play Harrow at Lords was Wellingtonian.

A. D. COLERIDGE: Joe, what d'you think of our
chances?
J. W. CHITTY: My dear fellow, we can't be beaten.

He became a Law Lord, and because he talked so much in court was known as Mr Justice Chatty.

There is another memory of Chitty in Captain Markham's account of schooldays at Westminster. Markham saw a football match played in Great Dean's

Yard between Westminster and Eton, and recalled Chitty 'standing with legs apart over the ball, shouldering us over right and left as we charged him . . .' This match must have been played with rules agreed for the occasion, which reminds us that Westminster and Eton football were very different, and made different contributions to soccer. The influence of Westminster's eventual eleven-a-side dribbling game, with a fixed goalkeeper and a three-man offside law, is obvious; that of the Field Game, through the Old Etonians who faced Darwen, is not, and requires more explanation.

A Field eleven does not have a goalkeeper. It is set up in a 2–2–7 formation with two long behinds, two short behinds and seven forwards. Today it has lost some features to modern Health and Safety concerns, but retains the 'rouge', a kind of points score, and its offside law. It is the offside law that determines the nature of the game. Only the forwards can be offside. They can be anywhere on the pitch, in front of or behind the ball, but to remain onside they must run past an opposing forward before they receive the ball. This is why the clearance kicks by the behinds are crucial: they must be long to give territorial advantage, and high, so that they are in the air long enough to give the forwards time to run past their opposite numbers into the onside positions.

A Field eleven is very different from a soccer team in its notion of how to work together. Field forwards must run together, stay onside together, run back to keep their opponents offside, and follow a dribbler. Short behinds must intercept forward rushes and dribble themselves, long behinds must show judgement and find space with their clearances.

To this extent the behinds show how much more the 1870s Scots and indeed Darwen backs and halves could influence the play. Under soccer rules so could a good forward, but there are so many runners around the ball that it is difficult for a Field Game forward to have huge individual influence until it comes to scoring a rouge. This occurs when a defending player puts the ball over his own by-line and an opponent touches down and claims the rouge, a score which offers fewer points than a goal but can still be decisive. Moments when the ball reaches the by-line, and players hover almost in slow motion to force a ricochet off an opponent, are an extraordinary contrast to the unceasing chase. The Field Game is neither as complex nor as dramatic as soccer, but it creates a captivating emotion, like seeing a classical freize come to life.

In today's Field Game one sees frequent headed clearances, but in the 1870s they would have been volleys, the player often leaping into the air to meet the ball. The Old Etonians were reported to have done exactly this in their 1882 FA Cup Final against Blackburn Rovers. The Field Game ball itself is slightly smaller than a soccer ball and historically was made by an Eton firm called Plummers. The game lasts an hour, and originated the change of ends at half-time, just as Harrow Footer began the toss of a coin to choose ends, and Cheltenham the system of two umpires and a referee. The Field Game reached its apotheosis in the years after the start of the House Cup Competition in 1860. In 1869 there were eighteen houses and by 1876 twenty-three, some run by Dames (women) and some by Tutors (men). A house that historically had been run by a woman was still called My Dame's even when it was subsequently run by a man, like William Evans, who ran Evans House: and Evans House is central to Field Game mythology.

Evans heroes

The story of Evans is told in *Annals of an Eton House*, an anthology of reminiscences edited by Major Gambier-Parry in 1907, a vivid picture of a world within a world. The house was taken over in 1839 by Samuel Evans, a drawing master. His son, William, was an Eton pupil who left to become a doctor, but was called back when his father ailed. In his middle age William was heartbroken by the death of his wife, and became reclusive, and the house was run in effect by his daughter Ann, who died in 1871, and thereafter by her sister Joan. William himself died in 1877, aged seventy-nine.

The Evans family had artistic friends and Dickens, Thackeray, the orientalist painter John Frederick Lewis and Lord Brougham were among those who would visit for breakfast.

Discipline in the house was entrusted to an oligarchy of four or five senior boys who became known as 'The Library', because that was where they convened. The collection of books itself was started in 1855, sixteen years after the Darwen Mechanics' Institute. Eventually there were house debating and musical societies, and charades and amateur theatricals in the hall. At mealtimes new boys took their seats at the lowest table and worked their way up over the years. There were silver spoons and forks and a glass of wine on Sundays, and if this sounds civilised there were protests as late as 1871 that boys leaned out of upper windows and threw water, pieces of cake and rotten duck eggs at passers-by. They had stone-throwing fights with locals, yelled Liberal slogans at general elections, and stole one another's butter, books and umbrellas; and cruel rituals for new boys were recalled by Herbert Gladstone, son of the great man, and himself a Home Secretary.

'Crossing the Line', recalled Gladstone, made boys sit on what looked like a seat but was a bath full of water, or sit on a table with a hole in it concealed by a sheet. Underneath was a boy with a pin.

When a former housemaid was interviewed for Gambier-Parry's book she said that boys playing passage football would never stop or move out of her way. Passage football was a regular occurrence on wet days and winter nights, as were racquets and Battledore and Shuttlecock in the hall. The din must have been appalling (the Evans family themselves lived across the garden) but the hall itself displayed the justification: military and tribal trophies sent back by past members, and above all the sporting cups won by the house.

Evans House ran three Field elevens, called House Eleven, Lower Boys and Lower Division, and Lower Boys. The school Field eleven practised together, and there was the School Kickabout, when large numbers went out and perfected the long kicking that was such a feature of the game, and tactically so vital. On top of this Evans House would practise together on their own ground. By 1862 all the houses had chosen colours and Evans seem to have worn any old trousers and red shirts with a skull and crossbones badge like that of the 17th Lancers, who had charged with the Light Brigade at Balaclava. The house butler, incidentally, was nicknamed 'Corporal' and had charged with the Heavy Brigade.

In short, Evans were a Field Game powerhouse, and between 1865 and 1875 won the House Cup six times, and were runners-up three times; the 1864 semi-final against Drury's was a bitterly disputed defeat, and the following year Evans beat them in the final.

Some notable men captained Evans Field elevens. In 1864 and 1865 there was W. S. Kenyon-Slaney, who played for Wanderers in the FA Cup Final of 1873, and for Old Etonians in 1875 and 1876, when there were four Evans men in the side. Hubert Parry, Keeper of the Field, captained Evans in 1866. Later he became the composer Sir Hubert and wrote the famous setting of Blake's 'Jerusalem', bellowed in our time at Labour Party conferences and the funerals of leftish intellectuals: a very Etonian sort of paradox.

But, then again, were not Old Etonian literary men like Cyril Connolly and George Orwell the ultimate scugs, who derided the games culture, and is not Orwell's unabashed realism a very Etonian mindset? And in Parry's ideal city, no doubt, and why not, there would be a playing field, and the relentless running of boys in red shirts with skull and crossbones badges.

After Parry there were interesting captains in the Lyttelton brothers: Edward, who became headmaster of Eton, and Alfred, who played both soccer and cricket for England, went into politics and was Colonial Secretary. As a fag in Evans House, Alfred had once tripped on the top of the stairs and sent a plate of steak and gravy flying on the passage floor. He picked it up, turned it over, put it back on the plate and served it; but he was rumbled and beaten. In 1874, writing as Keeper of the Field, Alfred gave an interesting sidelight. Arguing in favour of a free kick against people who loitered offside, 'sneaking', as it was called, he said that thirty or even twenty years earlier the game had been far rougher, and 'the remedy for the breaking of the rule was to kick the offender with sufficient vigour to prevent the recurrence of the offence. Such a remedy should if possible be avoided.'

Quite apart from what it says about retaliation, such a long memory of football enabled Evans men to create their own legend. In 1877 R. D. Anderson, a boy in the house who became secretary of the Old Etonian soccer club and played twice against Darwen, compiled *The Book of Evans Heroes* from sporting records going back to 1851, and another boy, J. K. Stephen, wrote under the pseudonym 'Ghost of Homer' forty lines of Greek verse entitled 'The Hurdles and Quarter of a Mile'.

More than thirty years later Gambier-Parry's book quoted Edward Lyttelton's remembrance of Evans's defeat by Madame de Rosen's in the House cup final of 1873, and it is a classic:

. . . the best House Eleven that I can remember lost the Cup. It was taken out of my Dame's late on a dark evening, wrapped in crepe, and the following day we received a black-edged postcard from my old friend Charles Lacaita, containing the well-known words of Herodotus on the defeat of the Persians, and with OTOTOTOTOTOTOI all across the card.

'OTOTOTOTOTOTOI' being the great lament when in the *Agamemnon* of Aeschylus, written in the fifth century BC, the warrior-king is found slain.

Their run of victories, and perhaps their hubris, did not make Evans popular. Their boys were not liked because 'they hung together very much'. Most of the school watched the cup finals, and Edward Lyttelton described the 'sullen silence that was sometimes almost general, even in the face of a brilliant performance, when an unpopular house was winning by the finest play . . . I should say that not even the modern school novel has exaggerated the excitement that prevailed. It was certainly excessive, and prejudicial to the unity of the school.'

'Football Mania', J. J. Riley was to call it; and Joan Evans, who once remarked that the de Rosen boys sharpened their boots before they played her house, sought to defuse the anti-Evans hostility by allowing boys who breakfasted with her to invite two friends from outside, and by herself entertaining various masters. She was a shrewd woman who, said Alfred Lyttelton, knew 'where mischief ended and wrong-doing began', and she never allowed a bad boy to remain until he was Head of House, but would always request his withdrawal. In her old age former house members subscribed to have her portrait painted by John Singer Sargent, an enquiring, dark, serious picture that she bequeathed to the College, who still own it.

Much to be deplored

At school level the problem of the Field Game was to find opponents, and as at Queen's Park everyday matches were between scratch teams. As late as the 1870s the ingenuity of these selections was considerable: Boats versus No Boats, North versus South, Dames versus Tutors, Those Who Shave versus Those Who Don't Shave, Those With 'A' In Their Names versus Those Without. After they left school it was easy for old boys who wanted to play soccer to find clubs, and men who wanted to carry on with the Field Game could find a way. At the beginning of the 1870s the school had many Field Rules fixtures against Old Etonians in other institutions: the Grenadier and Coldstream Guards, the Household Brigade, Christ Church and Balliol at Oxford.

Not for almost twenty years after the formation of the FA in 1863 was every soccer match in Britain played to exactly the same rules, and for years teams and even associations would compromise to get a fixture; and it must have been difficult for many to give up what had been habits learned at school. In the 1866/7 season Wanderers played Old Etonians in thick fog in Battersea Park and the Etonians could not resist a bit of Field Game handling: they had to be reminded that 'fives was a distinct game, and entirely separate from the game of football'.

As the 1870s progressed, however, the school was obliged to accept more fixtures against teams who would play Field Rules on condition that the return was under Association. An early example of this are games against the Royal Engineers in October and December of 1873, and it is difficult not to see here a deliberate attempt to promote soccer by Francis Marindin.

Marindin was forty-one when he kept the Old Etonian goal against Darwen. His family were Huguenots who settled in England 200 years earlier; his father was a West Country clergyman and his elder brother an Eton master. Marindin himself saw action in the Crimea and served in Aden and Mauritius. From 1869 to 1875 he was Brigade Major of the Royal Engineers at Chatham Depot, where he fashioned a formidable regimental team. In 1873 they went on the first football tour by an English club, visiting Sheffield and the Midlands. Heading the ball is said to have started in Sheffield, and in 1875 Lieutenant Sim, the Engineers' back, was the first man to head the ball in a Cup Final.

The Engineers won the Cup twice and in 1900 J. H. Catton wrote that they were the first English team to demonstrate the value of combination, in terms of 'concerted action and lining up'. Marindin was elected to the FA Committee in 1871 and by 1879 had resigned his commission and was Inspecting Officer of Railways for the Board of Trade. Later he was knighted and refereed eight Cup Finals. He kept unfussy control with quiet warnings: 'If you do that again I shall send you off the field.'

By insisting that one of a pair of fixtures be under Association rules, and by helping to re-found the Old Etonian club, Marindin sought to influence Etonians in two ways. The first was to make them think about soccer as the game they would have to play most when they left school. The second can be gleaned from the Field Book response to the re-formation of the Old Etonian club, which would of course be committed to soccer rules.

'It is to be hoped,' wrote M. B. Hawke, the Keeper of the Field, 'that all Old Etonians who are eligible for the club will now join it and give their earnest support, so that Eton may not be behind other Public Schools and that she may have a club worthy of herself. Floreat Etona.'

Pragmatism. Move on. If you can't beat them, join them and beat them that way. *Floreat Etona* indeed.

Hawke was the future Lord Hawke of Yorkshire and England cricket fame, and had a broad view of how sport might develop. Earlier Keepers of the Field had been critical of fixtures under soccer rules. In 1876 J. Wilson wrote that 'the effect upon the style of play was visible this year, and was much to be deplored. The Chatham match is a source of much of this evil and if it could be dropped without "giving offence" it would be a great point gained.' The Chatham match was the return soccer fixture against the Royal Engineers. The 1877 Keeper, G. K. Douglas 'endeavoured to play as few association matches as possible and to have no practice matches under their rules'.

Weaknesses of the Field eleven when playing soccer are given as: not being used to playing ninety minutes, a lack of practice when running back and dealing with long throw-in play, and 'tiring themselves out by running across the field instead of remaining at their posts'. In their first game in 1873 they 'never got the ball beyond half way and kicked too far'. They lost all their soccer games until they drew 2–2 with Remnants on 5 December 1878. A month earlier, and a week after their re-founding, Old Etonians beat the Field eleven 4–0 at soccer: it was a warm-up for their first round Cup tie a week later. Many of the Field players were new to soccer, wrote Hawke, and the Remnants team that drew 2–2 was different in personnel from that which played Darwen.

Despite that, the form lines are still there, and they show that Darwen had an uphill task: not least because somewhere in that use of the school eleven as practice fodder, and in the resentment at Evans House triumphalism, the glory of the Field had been diminished. It had also been bequeathed, not to schoolboys, but to grown men of the world who were determined to justify it and succeed.

Zulu winter

Overnight the Darwen team had become not just the local team but heroes, their hands shaken, their backs slapped, their healths drunk. They must have had stomach flutters at the thought of Old Etonians, and despite the ice and slush on the streets walked on air at the memory of Remnants. Some of them were on short time or laid off, all felt the pinch, and most of them must have had friends or neighbours who every day waited in line at soup kitchens. Darwen Rangers lost two matches to the frost, and most of the news was bad.

Local Liberal leaders who went to a big party meeting in Manchester were told by the veteran orator John Bright that 'the Afghan War is one of the most foolish in which the country has ever been engaged. It is a crime, and if possible a greater blunder, which will take the nation long to retrieve . . .'

Action in Afghanistan was a consequence of Disraeli's imperialist stance against the Russians, and so in another way was the Zulu War. The Colonial Office dreaded expenditure, but the Governor of the Cape Colony, Sir Bartle Frere, sensed the mood of the Tory leadership. Communications between him and London were carried by cable to St Helena, and by ship from St Helena to Capetown, which made rapid responses impossible. Both the Boers and the Zulus were pushing into empty territory, and Frere wished to hold both in check. This was before anyone knew that there were gold and diamonds in the Transvaal, and when Britain's fundamental interest was coaling ports on the way to India.

Frere cooked up a scheme whereby he would incite the Zulus to fight, defeat them, and impose a settlement. Before the Colonial Office could stop him he had despatched his troops, and on 22 January 1879 they were catastrophically defeated at Isandlwana. A Zulu commander now exceeded his instructions and entered notional British territory, where he was staved off at Rorke's Drift, a legendary stand that caught the public imagination and, whipped up by the press and music hall songs, inspired a jingoistic imperial patriotism.

It was surely more than Disraeli dared to dream, yet it was his curious outsider's instinct that had detected how the world was changing. As a young man he wrote novels about the 'Two Nations', the old rich and the new industrial poor, and was not his imperialism the false glue that would hold them together? In politically stalemated Darwen had not George Butterworth's Zulu Minstrel Quartet been a provincial sign of the times?

As a shocked public received news of the defeat at Isandlwana there was a weekend thaw. It enabled Darwen to beat Accrington 6–0, in what was an ideal warm-up for the Old Etonian tie. The first goal followed another free kick by Suter, and they passed beautifully and kept it well together, wrote J. J. Riley.

The Darwen Committee had pondered the first trip to London and arranged this one in a less tiring fashion. On Thursday, 12 February, the team left Darwen at a quarter to eight in the morning and arrived at their London hotel just after three. About twenty friends and supporters went with them. Other attractions in the capital that week included 'Trafalgar', a Grand Naval Spectacle with 'hundreds of specially trained boys'. Presumably the boys were arranged by size to give an illusion of distance, a famous old staging trick. Henry Irving was in *Hamlet* at the Lyceum, and at the Royal Academy there was an exhibition of Old Master drawings. At Kennington Oval, although nobody quite knew it yet, it was a question of who were to be the new masters.

Whom the gods love

Four years later, when substantially the same Old Etonian side were beaten 2–1 by Blackburn Olympic in the Final that settled the issue of soccer mastery, the Olympic players were said to have an average height of five foot six and weight of ten and a half stone: the Old Etonians were to a man two or three inches taller and from a stone to a stone and a half heavier. In 1879 they were described as the biggest lot of men that Darwen had played against, and the physical discrepancy was probably more or less the same as it was to be in 1883. Darwen were underdogs indeed, and not particularly pedigree, either.

Against this it was reported that Old Etonians were unable to field their best side because Alfred Lyttelton, Bury and Novelli were unavailable. Lyttelton had played once for England, when to a colleague who complained about not receiving a pass he made the famous rejoinder: 'Sir, I am playing purely for my own pleasure!' He played in four cricket Tests, and scored more than 4,000 runs for Middlesex. At football his chief asset was his pace.

In the mid-1870s he ran recorded hundred yards of 11 and 11.5 seconds, which is better than Darwen's Tommy Marshall's recorded 13 seconds. Straight races are not the same as running with the ball, of course, and Tommy may always have been attempting to deceive the handicapper.

Judging by what happened at first, and even allowing for the gale that blew from the gasometer end, the appearance of the Etonians who were available did disconcert Darwen: immaculate kit, Chitty-like self-confidence and legends of the football almanacks. Here in the actual, healthy flesh were the heroes whom the gods adored.

Marindin was in goal and captain. Arthur Kinnaird was the star personality of the age, as notorious for hacking, fouling and gamesmanship as he was active in the sort of hearty Christian causes that football was supposed to inspire. It was his mother Lady Kinnaird who said that she was worried that one day Arthur would come home with a broken leg, and according to which version of the tale one hears Alcock or Marindin who said, 'Don't worry. It won't be his own.' Kinnaird was thirty-two years old, had grown his beard while still at school, and his speech was loud, clipped and decisive. He had been very speedy, and played always in white cotton duck trousers and an Eton cricket cap.

Kinnaird's fullback partner, Christian, was two-footed, and a fair-haired man with generous features. His family were tea planters in Ceylon. H. H. Calvert was more used to playing back but appeared here at half. He was still at Trinity College, Cambridge, and later became a soldier. The other half was J. C. Welldon, a former King's scholar at Eton, who became head-master of Dulwich College and Harrow, and eventually

Bishop of Calcutta: photos show a big, solid, genial sort of person.

Wide right was J. B. T. Chevallier, who had weight and pace and was said to 'charge well'. He taught mathematics at Repton and Lancing before coming into his family's estate at Aspell Hall in Suffolk, where he revived the cider-making founded there in 1728 and bred red-poll cattle: like the Reverend Philip Graham of Darwen, who bred the same on his first wife's farmland. Chevallier's right-wing partner was H. M. Sedgwick, a Clapham Rovers player who rejoined Old Etonians. He was said to have a dead shot at goal, but to be 'a little averse to work'.

A. C. Bonsor played centre forward in the first game only. His strike partner was H. C. Goodhart, one of the stars of the era, whose fame endured among those who saw him. J. H. Catton, seeking in 1900 to describe the 1887 Preston Invincibles forward Fred Dewhurst, said that 'he was the Goodhart type, he could simply walk over opponents and did'. Tall, high-cheekboned, handsome, unselfish, always in front of goal when needed: the gods loved Goodhart and he proved the adage correct, because he did die young, at thirty-five, when Professor of Latin at Edinburgh University.

The left wing, H. Whitfeld, was another who rejoined the Old Etonians, in his case from Wanderers. He was an all-rounder who had won the school mile and run second in the Steeplechase, and made 2,400 runs for Surrey, whom he captained for a season. He was a good dribbler, very tall, with striking dark looks. He later became a Member of Parliament.

In the absence of Lyttelton, R. D. Anderson, the Evans boy who had just left school and was secretary of the club, played outside Whitfeld. His photos show a smallish, neat, earnest, big-eared person.

Christian, Kinnaird, Goodhart and Whitfeld were internationals, and the fact is that the re-formed Old Etonians had what we would call a first team squad of some twenty players, none of whom would lower the standard. Against this Darwen's Tommy Marshall and Brindle were to appear for England, W. Kirkham was clearly extremely skilful and Suter would have played internationals but for football politics. Darwen's strength in depth was to be called into question, as was the quality of the entire team without Suter: but on this day the main question was once more psychological.

No extra time

Charles Alcock was again to referee, and Tom Hindle was the Darwen umpire. The ground was soft but not sloppy, there was intermittent rain and the wind was so strong that journalists reckoned it to be worth one or two men extra. Old Etonians won the toss and chose to play with it behind them. They tried to run our men off at once, said J. J. Riley, and almost succeeded. In those days, when the ball was kicked out it was thrown in one-handedly by the side who grabbed it, and Kinnaird took devastating advantage.

Old Etonians rushed forward and although Suter and Brindle defended well there was only one Darwen break-out. They could not clear the ball. The Etonian backs kicked long with the wind, their huge forwards locked arms in upright scrimmages and kicked wide for the dribblers. One of Kinnaird's throws was soon carried by the wind into the mouth of the goal, where the ball touched Whitfeld and rolled in.

Darwen countered through Gledhill and W. Kirkham, but, when Marindin cleared, the ball went so quickly to the other end that Christian, following up through men who stood still to avoid being offside, was in the clear and scored. J. J. Riley said that when

Darwen had the odds against them 'they usually let their feathers droop, but on this occasion they plucked up in spite of wind and rain'. Marshall's pace took him ahead, he passed to Love and Love to Bury, who shot over.

At this point the wind increased and Old Etonians had all the play, scoring again after another huge throw by Kinnaird. Such were the confusions of scrimmages that *The Sportsman* gave the goal as a header by Novelli, who wasn't even playing. The *Darwen News* said Goodhart.

Neither is there a name to whoever pulled one back for Darwen, perhaps the most vital goal of the game, in that it was scored against the wind; and the manner of it is significant. The centres Gledhill and W. Kirkham passed the ball to the left and then to Marshall on the right. Marshall was said by Alcock to 'pass with judgement' and on this occasion he put in the scorer.

Old Etonians raised their game again: bulldozing runs by Goodhart and Chevallier, and, when they were halted, scrimmages to draw men in and release a Whitfeld dribble. Although Suter, according to *The Sportsman*, was especially cool and quick, Old Etonians scored again when Duxbury saved but at the expense of a corner, which Goodhart headed in. Worse was to follow when Goodhart made it 5–1: another long throw and another tall man's header. Half-time was then taken on the pitch, and to the small crowd of 200 it must have seemed that the game was decided.

What happened, however, seems as romantic today as it did at the time: by whatever determination not to be humiliated, by whatever dream of the game, by the coolness of Suter and the driving captaincy of Knowles, by details of play that showed imagination, an overhead kick by Dr Gledhill, a stoop by W. Kirkham so that the charging Bonsor 'rolled over him like a dead oxen', Darwen rallied and cut the deficit. It was a move that exemplified the passing game as opposed to that which held the ball in a scrimmage: a lateral move in which men ran in line and the ball went from R. Kirkham to Bury outside him, was screwed in to Gledhill and moved across to Jimmy Love, whose centre forced Welldon to head through his own goal. The rest of the match was entirely in Darwen's favour, but with fifteen minutes to go they were still three goals behind.

Then, as Riley wrote, 'never did they exhibit greater unity of action, greater energy and perseverance, and never were their efforts carried with more success than was the next ten minutes, for the passing and play was to such perfection that the three goals were obtained, through good passing and then scrimmage, much to the surprise of the Etonians who were utterly exhausted, to the amazement of the spectators . . .' The crowd scenes were wild and hats thrown into the air as Love scored with a header from a long Moorhouse throw, and then Alcock gave a classic decision to make it 5–4. The ball was forced in by a scrimmage (no one seems to know who last touched it), whereupon Kinnaird protested that since he had handled the ball before it went in the goal should be disallowed and a free kick awarded. It is not clear if he handled deliberately. The Darwen players replied that they had not appealed to the umpire against this offence, and the umpire had not appealed to the referee. Alcock agreed: no foul; the goal must stand.

With five minutes left Jimmy Love went through and equalised, and a man from Swinton, near Manchester, who happened to be in London on business, was so excited that he not only sprained his ankle but smashed his umbrella as well.

Both Remnants and Clapham Rovers had played extra time in recent ties but Marindin refused. His men were spent. Would they have played the next day? Nobody knows, because as Marindin must have been aware, Darwen's players, including Suter, Gledhill and Marshall, had to travel to Chester to represent the Lancashire FA. To Darwen it must have seemed like a victory, but the fact was that Old Etonians had got out of jail, and there would have to be a replay. This would entail another Darwen journey to London; unless, of course, the FA would allow the Old Etonians to be persuaded to go to Darwen.

Don't sock between times

Darwen's stamina played a big part against Remnants and their first game against Old Etonians, but we can only guess at their training routines. Once they left school, Gentlemen Amateurs seem to have kept fit by playing, and the Eton Field Book sometimes mentions 'want of condition' among their opponents. Indeed, the fact that covert professionals had time to train occasioned sneers against them, as at the FA's 1884 annual general meeting when N. L. Jackson asked if 'five years ago did they ever hear of a team training for a week or more prior to an engagement?'

'What about the Oxford and Cambridge boat race?' cried a voice from the back of the room, and it was a point well made.

Alcock's *Football Annual* editorials contain many interesting thoughts about how to play, and show how open-minded he was. In 1875 he thought it best to push down the centre towards the actual goal, but by 1884 he agreed that 'long passing to the extreme outside is often very effective'. He always preferred to see a man keep his balance ('your body well-set, your elbows tight') and avoid a charge when in possession, although he did make it clear that teams used charging to counter the early passing game, knocking men over as they received the ball.

At the same time he says nothing about training methods, and the best hints as to what people thought in the late 1870s are in *The Eton Game*, which was edited by James Doraime in 1902. The main text was a letter of advice written in 1897 by Doraime's father, who in the 1870s had been at Eton before him. Some modern wags have seen the letter as a coded warning against masturbation. Take a cold bath and go to bed early with the windows open, it says, but more to its point it warns that 'if you want to be a scug be greedy'. Do be regular. Don't sock (i.e. eat) between times. Stop potatoes and eat marmalade. Chew and eat slowly. The best way to pass the spare time in training, it says, which surely implies that there were periods of training before certain events, is to sing or read. Don't fug up a hot room. Don't rag, it ruins the digestion. A hot bath should consist of two cans of water, one hot and one cold. Outside you must wear a sweater and sweat. Dribble past a friend on the line. Exercise should last an hour: sprints that include a long, fast burst. Dog-trotting will only improve your wind.

In the early 1880s Blackburn Olympic went for a week to Blackpool, the event which spurred Jackson's question. They took brine baths, and their routine was a glass of port and two raw eggs first thing, a three-mile walk, porridge and haddock at breakfast, training on the sands, a leg of mutton at midday, porridge and a pint of milk at teatime, and six oysters apiece for supper. J. H. Catton wrote in 1900 that when the

Darwen outside left, Tom Bury, was asked if he would like a similar week he had replied, 'Nay, nay, it wud tak me weeks to get used to Blackpo. Give me a few extra buttercakes and let me have some long walks and I'll show 'em how Tom Bury can play.'

Clearly, we are at a rudimentary stage in these matters, when apart from something like the Eton Whole School Kickabout, training was not football-specific, but based on what men had done in pedestrianism and prize-fighting. Actual footballs were expensive, and a small recreational club like Darwen Rangers would try to save its ball for match days. So it may well be that an unfortunate trend began as early as the late 1870s. Certainly, a clever journalist like Catton was writing by the early 1900s that in his opinion English footballers did not practise enough with the ball.

It seems reasonable to assume that Tommy Marshall, who knew something about training, helped the Darwen players to achieve fitness, although when and how often they had time to train we do not know. Did someone like Suter work as well with the ball? The annuals all stress his technique, his two-footedness, accurate kicking and fine heading, as well as his speed, so presumably he did work at these things, and encourage others to do the same. He and Love would have learned good habits in Scotland, and so come to that would W. Kirkham.

Returned by a 'No!'

She was poor but she was honest, isn't it a blooming shame? It's the rich what gets the pleasure, it's the poor what gets the blame. So the Victorian song tells us, and as the Old Etonians versus Darwen saga continued into the month of March, sporting press editorials and readers' letters maintained the controversy. For the most part, Old Etonians were accorded both the pleasure and the blame: they had kept themselves in the tie by a cynical insistence upon the letter of the regulations, and then complained in letters and conversation that the opposing forwards always lay offside: a habit, one reader of the *Athletic News* who saw all the games pointed out, to which they were particularly prone themselves.

Darwen's posture was struck by the club secretary W. T. Walsh's letter to the *Darwen News*, in which he urged people to continue to support the Subscription Fund.

As times are bad and money scarce, we cannot expect any of our moneyed men to give us a treat to London. We are prompted to appeal to the general public for assistance, so as to enable the working lads of our own town to compete against government inspectors, university professors and noblemen's sons etc etc and whether we are conquerors or conquered we feel sure that the result will be an honour, not only to the club but to the town and county.

This is spin inspired by a sort of witty disgruntlement, the 'etc etc' being a very good touch. It invites the question of why the 'moneyed men' could not be relied upon, suggests somehow that they were no longer interested in local honour, and appeals to another sort of person; and perhaps to chips on provincial shoulders.

At street level, enthusiasm and the new phenomenon of people living their lives through support for a football team burst into poetry. It was more like doggerel than the Homeric stanzas of Evans House, but none the less heartfelt. The *Darwen News* published the following, above the pen-name 'A Darwen Lad':

The Darwen Football team to London did go
And played in a match which ended in a draw;
At half time they stood one to t'other team's five
But they put matters straight, how the ball
    they did drive!

The last fifteen minutes they did something in it
For they got three goals, now didn't they spin it?
Darwen wanted to play on for a half hour or so
But the answer was promptly returned by a 'No!'

A week earlier outdoor relief of bread and soup had been given to 326 people, at a cost to the borough of £21, and a woman named Joan Greenhalgh was given seven days for getting drunk, pulling off her clog and breaking six windows. Zulu War casualty lists were being published and on the day that A Darwen Lad's poem appeared it was reported in the *London Illustrated News* that Arthur Kinnaird and his father had each been left £1,000 as executors of a will.

Behind the scenes Darwen had offered Old Etonians £40 to come north and play at Barley Bank. Old Etonians refused but gave Darwen £15, to which the co-conspiring FA added £10. Neither the *Darwen News* nor the general press expanded at the time upon the secret financial problems involved but J. J. Riley showed that he understood them, when he printed without comment a motion submitted by Old Harrovians for discussion at the Annual General Meeting of the FA on 27 February 1879: it concerned professionalism and residential qualifications for membership of a football club. It was the first drop of rain that falls more or less ignored before a dark sky opens.

On the field, as both trade and actual skies brightened, the team maintained its good form. Church, old rivals but now not much more than a mill team, were beaten 7–0, and Bolton Wanderers 4–2. Football on the Bolton side of the moors did not improve as rapidly as on the Blackburn, evidence perhaps of the fiercer local patriotism of towns like Preston and Blackburn. They had been important when a place like Bolton was nothing, and they wanted to be recognised again, and Darwen itself had long believed in its own identity.

The man of muscle

Three hundred people were at Darwen railway station to see the team and a few friends leave in a special carriage of the Great Northern Railway for the Oval replay, which took place in beautiful, spring-like weather on Saturday, 8 March 1879. Darwen were unchanged, although the forwards were printed in the paper as being in different positions, with Gledhill wide right and Marshall wide left. Whether this is how they played, or is another example of the journalism of the time, which would quite often print names incorrectly, is impossible to say.

Old Etonians made three changes, which probably added strength. Calvert, Bonsor and the youthful Anderson, who instead acted as umpire, were replaced by L. Bury, C. J. Clerke, and Julian Sturgis. Sturgis, an Evans man who had figured in their cup teams, was a writer and barrister; Clerke was described as 'fast down a side, and a good shot', and Bury was a personality and one of the best players of the day. Big and darkish, he was known as 'the man of muscle', and praised for his sportsmanship. The Hon. Gilbert Coleridge, who played against Bury in the 1870s, wrote in 1912 that 'there were some long behinds who invariably managed to kick you as well as the ball . . . you might be kicked off your feet into the air and the ball would be between you and his toe.' But if Bury 'kicked the ball before you reached him the swing of his leg was checked like the spent string of a bow, and you never felt his foot'. Bury was nevertheless very strong, with a long and accurate kick. He became an orange grower in Florida. By coincidence James Christopher Ashton of Darwen was to fail in the same profession, and die as an expatriate in Atlanta, Georgia. To accommodate Bury, Christian moved up to his more accustomed halfback role; Sturgis and Clerke were both forwards.

Alcock refereed and W. T. Walsh was the Darwen umpire: it is remembered that Alcock followed Harrovian practice and looked around and called, 'Are you ready?' before he gave the signal to kick off at fourteen minutes past two. The play seems to have been tight and cautious and Old Etonians went ahead through Clerke. On the half-hour R. Kirkham equalised after a scrimmage.

So far as one can read from the reports there was a tactical battle in which Old Etonians sought to stop Darwen moving the ball wide by using their defenders Kinnaird and Christian in the scrimmage alongside Goodhart and Sedgwick, and keeping their other forwards wide to charge the Darwen quick men. Weight was their advantage, and they sought to use it. Darwen seem to have countered by putting Knowles into the scrimmage with Gledhill and the two Kirkhams.

We can imagine the scrimmage as a lot of leaning and shoving, with one side trying, as in a rugby scrum, to keep the ball within the forest of its own legs, and then release it. This must have been much more difficult with a soccer ball than with a rugby oval, which a foot can well and truly hook. On the other hand it must have been easier for a cheekily skilful man like W. Kirkham to nick the ball. That is why in the old days there was a lot of hacking to hurt and intimidate, and in the 1870s a lot of leaning and shoving in which superior weight was important. By 1879 all teams played the 1–2–2–6 formation, but the Etonian forwards, true to their Field game and inherited historical instincts, still hunted more as a pack. Darwen tried to play more in a line, to which the Etonians clearly sought answers. Within a few years, it was to be the line that prevailed.

In the second half a familiar routine put Old Etonians 2–1 up, when from a scrimmage the ball went to Whitfeld, who dribbled on to score. Entertaining was the word used to describe the play thereafter, and when Darwen got a passing movement going Gledhill made the equaliser for Tom Bury. On this occasion Old Etonians agreed to extra time, as well they might, but it did not break the deadlock, and it finished 2–2.

Again Darwen asked Old Etonians to travel north, and again the answer was returned by a 'No!' So Darwen went home, knowing that they must come back the following Saturday, and the newspapers heaped more scorn upon their adversaries.

'Whatever satisfaction it may be to the Old Etonians that they have compelled the Darwen club to spend this large sum of money they are heartily welcome to,' grumbled the *Athletic News*. 'Doubtless on some hands it may be hard to appreciate the feeling which activated the Darwen people . . . but in Lancashire and Yorkshire these displays are neither rare nor uncommon. There is a hearty love of genuine and honest sport of all descriptions . . .' A material blow was that W. Kirkham was injured, and would have to be replaced by McLachlin. Kirkham was twenty-four years old and the injury ended his career.

1,230 miles

Psychological wear and tear is as much a killer as physical where replays and double legs are concerned, and Darwen suffered from both. Within the week the weather improved and more cotton mills returned to full-time working. Players who had been laid off or were on short time needed their wages. The consequence was that for the third match against Old Etonians the Darwen party left for London neither the day before nor in the special carriage, that in their heads, maybe, had been a triumphal car to victory. This time they travelled overnight, after a full day's work, sitting upright, half waking and body-clocks disturbed. Is this surprising? It is, and there was surely more to it than mill wages or cost-saving by the club.

J. J. Riley wrote that the FA Cup run assumed 'gigantic proportions' and it is as though these proportions had become too great, and the mental and emotional journey had reached a point of exhaustion. Players, officials and the public, many of whom had given money they could barely afford, when men who could afford plenty had given nothing, all wanted a conclusion: and it could be any conclusion so long as it was one. Either that, or they believed

that come what may they could never be beaten.
But the knack of knowing how to win despite everything is the Evans House lesson that Darwen, alas,
were too much the underdogs to learn. Even when,
after their all-night journey, they arrived at the Oval,
whatever rhythm they had expected was dislocated
by the fact that one of the Old Etonians did not
arrive on time because of a railway breakdown. Could
or should this have been disputed, and the match
started on time none the less, as Darwen had started
without Dr Gledhill at the very beginning of the
adventure?

Darwen's umpire this time was Tom Hindle, secretary of the Lancashire FA, anxious as an administrator
to get on with Alcock and Marindin and Kinnaird,
and here he was, a 24-year-old provincial, hob-
nobbing with grandees. Did he think it politic to
agree that the start must be delayed, when the bolshier
W. T. Walsh may well have resisted? Could or should
Alcock have insisted that the match start on time?
Nobody knows, or ever can know for certain.

But we may speculate. Within weeks of this second
replay there were arguments in Lancashire newspapers
about whether certain players were or were not paid
professionals, yet it was two or three years before
administrators like Alcock raised the issue. Can we
really believe that they did not know what was
happening? Were there no suspicions, no talk, no
gossip, no knowledge of the provincial press, no
involuntary but revealing remarks? A conspiracy of
silence suited Tom Hindle, no doubt, but it must
have suited the gentlemen as well. If they shut their

eyes to what was happening to their wonderful world of grown-up schoolboys, maybe whatever was nasty would go away.

For the second replay Old Etonians again made changes. Chevallier, Sturgis and Welldon dropped out, Anderson, Burrows and Edgar Lubbock took their places, and the team was shuffled positionally. Kinnaird played up front, Christian dropped back again, and Lubbock was at halfback. Some of these changes were caused no doubt by life's other engagements and events, but it is difficult not to see a deliberate strategy of meeting Darwen's skilful but much smaller players with men of greater power and a more phys-ical style of play.

From this point of view Lubbock was another Etonian classic, who had blown his top in the 1866 run-out dispute at Lords. Now thirty-two years old, he was the youngest of eight brothers, tall, with crinkly hair parted in the middle, and an air of easy superiority. He was already a partner in Whitbread's Brewery, and became a director of the Bank of England. A sporting all-rounder, and eventual Master of the Blankney Foxhounds, he was runner-up in the 1880 Wimbledon Tennis Championship, and for Eton and Kent had bowled 'a fast left underarm with a good deal of break'. His older brother, Robin, had a Field Game philosophy of 'Smash, dash and at 'em!'

For all the pressure and disruptions Darwen began the match well but failed to capitalise. They hit a post, and narrowly missed other chances. Then Knowles was injured. He seems to have stayed on but it was the turning point. Goodhart put Old

Etonians one up and Clerke made it 2–0 after a breakaway dribble from Sedgwick. Suter pulled one back from a corner by Marshall, but Sedgwick scored again and at half-time it was 3–1.

The second half was a disappointment of a kind that we all experience: on the day we are numbed and events seem to happen in another time and to someone else: the pain comes later. In brief, Sedgwick made it 4–1 and Whitfeld five. Marshall sprinted away on his own to score a solo, but Goodhart added a sixth for Old Etonians, and the underdog dream was over.

Having travelled some 1,230 miles, having displayed skill and resilience, having experienced in so short a time so many emotions, were Darwen really inferior by four goals? Yet how could they prove now that they were not? By their optimism, we may guess, and their boyish football team jokes as they went home. We know now that Darwen's historic moment had passed, but they, then, did not. Football Mania still raged. We'll be back, they would have said. Despite everything we'll be back next year and show them. Aren't we the best team in Lancashire?

Not a penny spent unnecessarily

Darwen were famous. They were the cock ducks, as the Lancashire saying has it. They were everybody's target and without realising it they and their local enemies had entered the modern world of ambition, expectations and money. But they went on as though nothing had changed. On 29 March five of their men represented the Lancashire FA against Cheshire and a week later Suter was said to be 'irrepressible' when on 5 April, without Gledhill, Love and the injured W. Kirkham, Darwen beat a Blackburn Association XI in pouring rain.

The ball itself became soaked and was replaced. The tape used instead of a crossbar, said J. J. Riley, 'hung between the shaky poles like the wings of a flabber-gasted chicken'. The forwards, he thought, passed too much instead of shooting, but the first of the real stories was his publication of the Final Accounts of the Fund to send the team to play in London.

Net proceeds of the benefit concert were £45 15s. 0d. and of the Subscription Fund £107 14s. 4d. The club's share of Cup gate receipts was £31 1s. 2d. versus Remnants and £87 0s. 10d. for the three Old Etonian games. This includes donations from the FA and the Old Etonians and gives overall income of some £270. But expenses had run high. The first two trips to London cost £61, with the club paying for eleven players and an umpire each time; and as the *Darwen News* wrote, 'every economy was used, not a penny being spent unnecessarily or on intoxicating drinks'.

What this means is that if we set actual match receipts of about £118 against travel costs of say £120 the financial situation without the fund-raising would have shown a very small loss; although cash in hand would have been needed to fund the original journeys. In other words the immense spin-doctored campaign and the desire to bring a replay to Darwen were as much about debt as affordability.

Then imagine a replay in Darwen. There would have been no travel costs, a crowd of at least 5,000 and extra brewery wagons, no doubt, for people who wanted to pay more to have a better view. The team's finances would have gone into the black, and they may well have won and earned more from the semi-final. As it was, Darwen still had debts from the levelling of the ground and would have to spend more to maintain the standard at which they found themselves. They were already running to stay where they were, and when they built a grandstand in the early 1880s they did not have the capital: the structure would always belong to the company who built it.

An interesting comparison here is that the turnover of the Football Association itself in 1879/80 was £329 3s. 2d. only some £50 more than that of Darwen, except that the FA had a balance in favour of £157 17s 6d.

The difference between these finances and those of a local recreational team is shown by the fact that the Singleton brothers' Darwen Rangers had an annual income of about £10. This included the sale of Rule Books, and for their April fixture against Darwen Reserves a share of the expenses and gate money. The match was bad-tempered and the Reserves' captain, Abraham Hayes, wrote to the *Darwen News* to justify his behaviour: 'As for my language being more terrible than polite, I deny having said anything that was not justified. I certainly used nothing like some of the language used by the Rangers to our Umpire when he said he had blown his whistle for offside . . .'

If this reads like something drafted by the club secretary it probably was, and for it to be written at all, talk in the town must have been rampant. It was an 1879 version of Wayne Rooney swearing at TV cameras, and more was to come, over an Easter of bitter rivalries, and an acrimonious close season.

PART THREE

Blackburn Rovers

Never mind the ball

When in November 1875 seventeen young men met at the St Leger Hotel in Blackburn and formed the Rovers, it seemed a similarly modest start in life to those other clubs Turton, Darwen Rangers or the St Luke's Sunday School Club that became Bolton Wanderers. In fact it was different, because the young men were different. Most of them had been to Blackburn Grammar School, where one, T. J. Syckelmoore, was a master. In the 1860s informal football was among various games played in the hard-cindered yard, but it seems to have lost out to cricket: by the mid-1870s there were regular organised cricket matches against other Lancashire schools.

It had become the local fashion, however, to complete a boy's education by sending him away to board for a couple of years, and like the Kays and Walshes and Hornbys they came home with a passion for the game. Of the founders and future players, Arthur Constantine was sent to Shrewsbury, Greenwood and the Hargreaves brothers to Malvern. The blue and white quartered shirts still worn by the Rovers were taken from those of Malvern College, except that Malvern wear green and white. 'Doc' Greenwood, the great Rovers fullback, always remembered the advice of his Malvern house captain: 'Go for the man and never mind the ball.'

The Rovers were made up of solid, educated, intelligent middle-class business and professional people, determined to get on and do things well. In the town they were seen at first as a gentlemen's club, and not as popular as the working-class Blackburn Olympic. Greenwood's family was in cotton, like that of Richard Birtwistle, who scored the club's first ever goal, against Church in December 1875. Walter Duckworth's father was a timber merchant, Birch was the son of the vicar of Blackburn and the Hargreaves brothers of the Coroner. Fred Hargreaves, described as 'a smart and active half-back', was to row for Oxford in the 1880 Boat Race. The famously outspoken vice-president of the club, the velvet-coated, cigar-smoking Dr Morley, was the son of a local medical family. His elder brother, John, became the first Viscount Morley of Blackburn, a writer and statesman, friend and biographer of Gladstone, colleague of Asquith and Lloyd George, and eventually Secretary of State for India.

From the start Rovers had the approval of wealthy men who were to become shareholders, and they proved to be canny about money and how to improve. Their first years show finances like those of Darwen Rangers. In 1875 they had an income of £2 8s. 0d. and in 1876 of £8 12s. 6d., which included 6s. 6d. in gate money. In December 1876, a sign surely of social confidence and ambition, they paid a policeman fourpence to regulate a small crowd. In the summer of 1877, inspired no doubt by Darwen's FA Cup entry, they upped their ambitions, and this coincides more or less with the return of John Lewis as a regular player. Maybe he had learned what he could from Darwen.

Rovers decided that they would need a better ground, one that was enclosed and had a better playing surface, and took the winter rent on a cricket field at Alexandra Meadows, next to the grammar school. They charged spectators sixpence and a shilling, more than Darwen's threepence, and only cut the entrance money when they were successful and knew that they could attract more people. Blackburn's population was three times that of Darwen, and the demographics were on their side.

At the same time, no doubt through Lewis, who had played for Darwen against Partick, they arranged fixtures with the Scots when they came south; and one of the letters that J. J. Riley ran in his sports newspaper was from the Partick captain, James Campbell. He complained that a Rovers goal had been scored when the Partick goalkeeper spilled the ball because he was pulled to the ground rugby fashion.

So Rovers played hard, and they began to go after working-class talent to improve the team. Tom Dewhurst, the weaver who gave the cross-field pass from which Yates scored Blackburn Olympic's winner in the 1883 Cup Final, said in later life that Rovers tried again and again to poach Olympic's players. Interestingly, several of the working-class youngsters Rovers did attract went to the same school: St John's Elementary, whose headmaster arranged sports even though the Education Act did not oblige him to do so. Altogether, the rise of Blackburn Rovers is the first instance of what we see in today's big European clubs: more income equals more success, equals more income etcetera.

Well marshalled by McIntyre

Easter Saturday 1879 fell on 12 April. A cold north-easterly blew across Barley Bank and there was a snow shower during the game. Blackburn Rovers, said the *Darwen News*, were envious and jealous of the honours showered upon Darwen, and the team that they brought was youthful, with a mixture of middle-class and working men, and one significant addition.

The previous Saturday, Suter's pal Hugh McIntyre of Glasgow Rangers had played for Scotland at Kennington Oval. It was his only cap, because the Scots would not pick men who moved to England. The *Darwen News* called him 'the finest half-back player in the Kingdom', and now here he was in Blackburn, with a new job as an upholsterer (although he was soon set up as a publican) and a new, ambitious team to mastermind.

Suter, out of sorts with a boil on his neck, put through his own goal in a 2–1 Rovers victory that showed where the future lay. McIntyre was the star. He marshalled his men well, and near the end booted the ball clean out of the ground when his defence was under pressure. This is probably the first recorded instance of row z professional defending. McIntyre's general attitude, and indeed the ill-will between the clubs, can be gathered from an incident in the following season. Darwen's goalkeeper, Duxbury, had to be attended on the field by his own centre-forward, Dr Gledhill, and then carried off because McIntyre 'in a most brutal and clearly a most unwarrantable ungentlemanlike and ungamelike manner had basely and foully charged him in a vital place'.

That was the future. About the 2–1 defeat the *Darwen News* was miffed and said that there was 'no special display of superiority by Rovers'. J. J. Riley said that Darwen were casual and not very good. At one point the Darwen forwards charged the Rovers keeper into the goal, but Rovers players shouted 'Not through!' and the keeper cleared. The Darwen umpire gave a goal, the Rovers umpire said not, the referee 'who was as far off as midfield also gave it in as no goal'. J. J. Riley was sure that 'a referee would do far better not to give his decision when he is half the length of the field away'.

The remarks of Blackburn's travelling support were described as 'coarse, vulgar and plentiful', and at the end of its report the *Darwen News* almost threw away its understanding that McIntyre 'is engaged as professional by the Rovers'.

This statement, when the paper came out, caused a furore.

Over £40 in threepences

On Easter Monday, Blackburn Olympic were Darwen's visitors and brought with them many supporters, including three women with large umbrellas that had OLYMPIC on them, and were to be opened in the event of victory. It was not to be. Darwen composed themselves and won 8–2. Olympic, wrote Riley, 'lacked those dodging powers which are so very useful in keeping off the enemy and staving away danger until assistance arrives'. Suter and Moorhouse, who although he was small was two-footed and very reliable, were praised for their skills in this area.

In contrast to Riley's report, the *Darwen News*, smarting from Saturday's defeat, wrote about both games as though Rovers had been fluke winners. Although Darwen were the heavier and more experienced team, Olympic showed 'more scientific knowledge of the game' than Rovers. Olympic were a junior club of only eighteen months' standing, but they had managed to carry off the Blackburn Association Cup. They are better than Rovers but we thrashed them would seem to be the subtext.

Riley, one feels, was the cooler judge, and noted that the £40 gate from the Olympic game 'was for the benefit of the Darwen players'. This surely confirms that benefit matches were a form of professionalism to which no one in the Lancashire area took exception. The Rovers gate had been £25, and an estimated 7,000 people saw the two matches.

Emigration

Two days after they played Olympic the Darwen first eleven and a few of their friends met in the Greenway Arms to say farewell to their captain, James Knowles. He was twenty-two years old and had decided to go to America. John Duxbury presided at a little ceremony at which Jimmy Love, as the oldest player, presented Knowles with a gold watch, guard and pendant. Thomas Bury said that they could not have had a better captain, and that without him they would probably have lost against Remnants. R. Kirkham, Edward Taylor and James Yates also spoke.

There had been Emigration Offices in Darwen since the Cotton Famine and Knowles was going out with the Mormon church. There was presumably a religious conviction on his part, and the Mormons were particularly efficient and reliable. They had group deals with shipping companies and always sent an Elder to take charge of the party.

On Wednesday Knowles said adieu to his team, and on Saturday he left Liverpool, in a ship called the *Wyoming*, with 170 others under the guidance of Elder Charles W. Nibley. They arrived in New York on 30 April and by 8 May were in Salt Lake City. From there Knowles moved to Payson, a farming community some sixty miles away. In 1899, when he was forty-two, he married the 27-year-old Mary Matilda Rasmussen, who had been born in Minnesota. He died in Payson in December 1928, aged seventy-one.

Football Mania

Knowles was leaving Liverpool when in the return game 4,000 people saw Darwen win 3–1 at Blackburn Olympic, and he was in mid-Atlantic when controversy blazed in the papers. J. J. Riley's eye for the ludicrous was ever keen, and in his match report he lambasted the Olympic committee and advised them to buy more than one football: 'Folks do not like to see a lot of the interest taken away from a match on account of the ball being half busted, and that only about the size of what we see lads kicking about in the streets . . .'

It was in the same edition of his short-lived sports paper that he described the state of Darwen, and of its team:

Darwen this season has been affected by a kind of 'Football Mania' and there happens to have been no life in the town, only that caused by football. Its Town Councillors have been twice elected without a contest – nay, with exceeding difficulty to make up the numbers. Several public officials have been appointed even without their consent.

The two political parties are almost dead, and, in fact, only appear to exist through their respective number ones.

While all this sleepiness is going on the rates of the town are reported to be much heavier than any other town in the district and twice the amount of Manchester. Darwen would do well to waken up or be born afresh . . .

We are under the impression that Darwen football club are following the same trend.

They appear to have a good eleven, but if one of them was unable to join in a match they could not find an equal substitute to fill the vacancy. It is evident in our own minds that they are tied up to an odd man.

In London, Old Etonians, having disposed of Nottingham Forest in the semi-final, fielded eight of the men who faced Darwen when they beat Clapham Rovers 1–0 in the Cup Final itself, and in Lancashire Blackburn Rovers launched an onslaught of letters to the papers. The club secretary, Walter Duckworth, denied that in the Easter Saturday game the Rovers goalkeeper had been shoved over the line, and H. Ibbotson, the Rovers umpire who had been criticised as 'not up to the goal by a considerable distance', demanded that Riley reprint 'the name of the official who after leaving the field stated that the goal claimed by Darwen but disallowed by the referee was a goal'.

Had TV replays been available this incident would clearly have been shown again and again, with pundits drawing circles around the positions of referee and umpires, and computer magic that would tilt the image to show events from their point of view. But if H. Ibbotson seems even at this distance in time to have been guilty and blustering, John Lewis, honorary treasurer of the Rovers, knew that the best form of defence is attack. He complained that 'a very nasty slur is brought against them [i.e. Rovers] and against Mr McIntyre, that he is engaged as a professional to the Rovers. Now this I flatly deny and beg to say that he has not, nor will he receive any money for playing for us. He is working in the town, and has been since he came.' He went on to say that four of the Rovers were under nineteen and one under seventeen, and 'if they will pull together they must naturally have a very brilliant future before them'. This was very true, particularly when in the autumn of 1880 he poached Suter to play at the back.

The most interesting question, though, is why were men like Lewis and Hindle ashamed or unwilling to admit to professionalism?

Respectable men degraded

The original FA Rules make no mention of professionalism because no one envisaged it: so, strictly speaking, until professionals were banned in the summer of 1882 it was not illegal to be paid. But to what extent was it unthinkable, and why?

Earlier in the century, in the world of wagers, cock-fighting, bare-knuckle pugilism and bear-baiting on the moors above Darwen, a baronet named Sir John Astley had run against all comers for side-stakes: he once went to Spain, even, and challenged any man in Madrid at a hundred yards. 'An amateur meant a gentleman,' he said of his day, 'whether he ran for honour or money or both.'

Astley had competed against professionals, Eton and Harrow boys had engaged professionals to bowl and coach cricket, A. N. Hornby strode out to bat with one, and as secretary of Surrey County Cricket Club Charles Alcock negotiated cricketers' wages and the beginnings of a regulated career structure. Cricket clubs like Darwen hired professionals, and offered prize money for sprint handicaps and football mini-tournaments. Yet Hindle and Lewis denied that any of their footballers were paid. Why?

Why did W. H. Jope, a representative of the

239

Birmingham Football Association, and a bitter opponent of paid footballers, say in 1884 that it was degrading for respectable men to play with professionals? What did he mean by respectable? What did professionals do that respectable men did not?

Victorian respectability, like today's political correctness, was an enforced social consensus to make people do the right thing, which in the aftermath of the Industrial Revolution was to be clean, sober, literate, industrious, God-fearing, respectful and monogamous. Churches preached respectability, governments legislated for it, and later generations mocked it, but at the time millions tried to embody it because it was a standard, which enabled them to improve and think well of themselves. Respectability seemed to many people to be the force that had cleaned up places like Dirty Darren and made life better, and who is to say that they were wrong?

So it is very easy to see why men like Tom Hindle and Thomas Duxbury, who had striven so hard to make something of themselves, would be impressed by their social superiors and want their approval. Easy, as well, to understand that gentlemen amateurs who had money and played football according to ideals as ridiculous as those of Don Quixote, actually, would be sad to see their paradise lost. Yet the anger and hatred that professionalism incurred, the undefined bile and hostility, went far beyond disapproval of the usual targets: betting, drinking, brawling and so forth.

It is as though people sensed somehow that professional footballers represented a social change too far, and did not know how to react. Why it was footballers who incurred this venom it is hard to know. Because they were heroes of a new kind of mass culture? Because they represented a change brought about by the purchasing power of the workers? Is this why there is something both heroic and shocking about Fergus Suter, and his self-possessed, realistic, level stare into the early team photo cameras? Here I am, he says. I am seeking to improve my life, and I am doing it by asking for money to play football. So I do not pretend to be a stonemason. Take me or leave me. Thank you.

His originality clearly nonplussed people at the time because decades later someone like J. H. Catton still wrote about it as though it was a surprise. Suter did not pretend. His position was a moral one. Later admissions like that of William Sudell, the cotton mill manager who masterminded Preston North End, and told an FA committee that of course he paid his players, were made in public and in effect made legalisation in 1885 inevitable. But they were political ploys. What Suter did was be himself.

Men like Alcock and Marindin and Kinnaird ignored professionalism while they could, but they had been educated to rule and to direct social change when necessary. Football rules, from 1863 to FIFA's banning of the tackle from behind in 1994, have always come about not as pure revealed wisdom, but in response to unfairness, cheating and violence. When Kinnaird was on the field he bent the rules as far as he could, but as an administrator he recognised that the Darwen ties made it imperative to clarify the situation regarding Cup venues and extra time. And however much Alcock regretted the loss of his gentleman amateur world he soon saw that 'the spread of the game depends upon professionalism', and was a leader in securing its acceptance.

In this Alcock resembled the England cricket captain the Hon. Ivo Bligh, who on his successful 1882–3 tour of Australia insisted that his amateurs and professionals (who included Hornby's Lancashire partner Dick Barlow) travel first class together, and this at a time when the amateur W. G. Grace would demand more in expenses than the professionals received in wages. In 1890 Marindin withdrew from football because he disliked professionalism, but he never vilified working men in public, nor questioned their morals.

This was the tactic of people from Sheffield and Birmingham whose football had been overtaken by ambitious and entrepreneurial Lancashire, and whose responses to change were not practical but emotional and morally indignant. As time went by and the strength of their own game declined, many southern amateurs and opinion makers were likewise not reconciled to professionalism and resented it in a most damaging way.

A shilling a week

Anti-professional rage was class-biased and out of proportion, but it is interesting that although there were gasps at the occasional rumoured bung, like that Suter seems to have received when he joined Blackburn Rovers, there were no objections to the actual level of wages. This is probably because they were more or less the same as the wages of professional cricketers in the late 1870s. These would be something like £5 for each three-day county game or about £80 for a season. A cricketer picked for the Players against the Gentlemen would receive £10. Since 1872 there had been residential qualifications to stop inter-county poaching. A maximum wage was not imposed on footballers until 1901, but on the eve of the First World War top players were on £4 a week plus winning bonuses.

Some of these players, like Meredith and Bloomer and Charlie Roberts, were entertainers whose fame endures to this day, but their money was not in essence more than that of a mill overlooker. Tommy Marshall made about £40 a year at Walmsley's Mill and an overlooker probably twice that. If Jimmy Love was paid for his factory job it was presumably at the normal rate, with football benefit money on top; and when Suter visited George Walsh for money it is unlikely that he received more than an overlooker, although he also received benefits and prizes at galas. The 'personal reasons' which led him to join Blackburn were presumably about a level of pay or a lump sum that Darwen would not match.

But he was a star and paid accordingly. Others had less negotiating strength. Mr Kerr, the mill owner employer of most of the Church team, paid the players a pound a week each plus legitimate expenses. When a Lancashire FA enquiry into professionalism sat at Bolton a Turton player named James Haworth said, 'I was made professional for a shilling a week. If we played away they sometimes gave us two and six for our tea as well.'

'What did you do with your shilling a week?' asked a panel member.

'I got six pints and got shut on't,' replied Haworth.

Clubs along the Bolton–Blackburn fixture list railway line seem to have paid tea and travel money from the start. Anything to keep the best players. In Sheffield the Association debated as early as 1867 a suggestion that clubs should pay for time lost from work, but it was rejected. It was, after all, the year of the Royal Commission on the Outrages.

After the 1885 legalisation of professionalism there was a rush to hire players, but it was hardly a bonanza to compare to today's TV money. Dodgy agents were, of course, in operation, and William Sudell was cherry-picking top Scotsmen to build a Preston team to rival Blackburn Rovers. Importation was seen in Glasgow as a scandal, but is perhaps better understood as an aspect of the economic migration from Scotland that went on throughout the nineteenth century.

In fact most professional footballers received wages that were decent enough for their social class but no more. The success of the game was an irrevocable change, but the lives of its players were still those of ordinary, uneducated working men. They had days of glory, but then what? Hugh McIntyre was restless after he left football, tried his luck in America, but came home, his life not radically improved. That Fergus Suter made a success of managing pubs, married a bit above himself and was able to retire in modest comfort is another tribute to his qualities, and an exception to the norm.

A benefit for Love and Suter

Between 1,500 and 2,000 people were at Turton's Chapeltown ground on 26 April 1879, to see Darwen beat Turton 7–2 in what was described as 'a match arranged for the benefit of Messrs. Love and Suter, the two Scotch gentlemen who have played with Darwen during the past season'. This was blatant professionalism, and yet at the same time it was an established local tradition.

The previous year Darwen had played a benefit for W. T. Walsh when he was laid off work, and a few days after the Turton game 200 spectators paid to see Blackburn Olympic Reserves play Hollin Grove (very likely a mill team) to help Edward Taylor, who had broken his leg. Whether this was the Edward Taylor who spoke at Knowles's farewell party is not known. But cricketers had benefits and so did footballers. Nobody seems to have given it a second thought, any more than they did to the fact that the Darwen Temperance Brass Band, a fanfare of respectability, played at galas at which men competed for money, bets were almost certainly laid on the side, there were probably beer tents and almost certainly hip flasks were in use in the pavilion.

Incidentally, the *Darwen News* reported a ridiculous event in the Turton game when a home player lay on the ball sooner than lose it in a scrimmage, 'and other players joined him on the floor'. The Eton Field Game had a rule against this, but soccer, having so it thought moved on, did not.

It was also the last match in which Jimmy Love appeared for Darwen, and fittingly enough he scored after a trademark dribble from midfield. After this he disappears from the story, in which he has been the most elusive of the major characters. There is no known photo of him, and no gossip. According to anecdote he is supposed to have joined the Navy – no one knows why – and to have been killed in the bombardment of Alexandria in 1882. This action saw eleven casualties in the British fleet, and Love does not figure in the published lists. The only clue is in the Marine Deaths Indices for 1883, in which a seaman whose name is entered as Jas. Love died aboard the battleship HMS *Triumph*. The *Triumph* had been at Alexandria but was refitted, and became flagship of the Pacific Fleet. So Love was committed to that vast ocean, perhaps, a shadowy, unknown and yet historic person.

The best team in Lancashire

The season's last reported game was played at Turton, between a Manchester and Bolton Eleven and a Darwen and Blackburn Eleven, and Suter was greatly praised. He 'fairly non-plussed Kerr just as the latter was about to make a straight shot at goal'.

What would the Darwen eleven be worth, asked J. J. Riley, if minus Suter?

There is a desire to whip up controversy and circulation in much of what Riley wrote, and yet his opinions ring true for two reasons: because events fell out much as he understood them, and because we see much of what he described in our own day. Darwen supporters, he wrote, have 'a reputation for bad behaviour and partiality, and are well-known for their complete blindness to the merits of any team but their own . . . If Darwen lose a thousand and one excuses are in vogue – the winners have had good luck and Darwen bad, the latter team was out of form, or were drunk, or were bribed by a well-known bookmaker to throw the game over . . .' Since the addition of McIntyre, Riley wrote, Rovers could fairly claim to be the best team in Lancashire, and he hoped that they would not think too soon about entering the FA Cup. Until they could carry it off it would be a wild goose chase, an opinion that was probably too cautious.

Yet Riley had seen it all, had he not, everything that the Evans House paladins saw, and that we continue to see: the Football Mania, the beauty and the unpleasantness; and, like us, he continued to be fascinated.

As a sort of ironic postscript he ran in what seems to have been the last issue of his sports paper an anonymous reader's letter. As an old provincial newspaper hand I would reckon him to have penned it himself, sitting in the office with a smile on his face. It read: 'Sir, I have never before had hold of a more bigoted and one-sided and unfair paper.'

But it does not say which side, and there's the clue.

Upright and guy-ropes

On New Year's Day, 1880, Old Etonians atoned for their churlishness and went to Darwen and played a friendly. They were beaten 3–1, Kinnaird and all, in sight of India Mill, where the Claude Lorrains had hung. Afterwards James Walsh hosted a dinner at Orchard Bank and made a graceful speech. As a Harrow man, he said, he rarely spoke well of Etonians, but today he could do no less.

Within months the house was sold and became the Alexandra Hotel, home pub for the team, and although George Walsh stayed in Darwen both James and Charles moved away. There were never many people in the Darwen mill-owning elite, and their richest man, Eccles Shorrock, Jr, never did put money into the football club. He was soon to be sued by his brothers for business negligence. When he lost he tried to appeal to his workforce, but was bundled out of Darwen with his legs sticking out of the window of a cab, and taken to one of the mental hospitals, from which he never returned.

Professionalism was begun by Darwen and it destroyed them. Without wealthy support they did not have the numbers to sustain it. Twenty years after the Oval Cup ties the original club was bankrupted, dissolved, and its replacement of no significance. Yet after the miraculous 1879 season there were still a couple of moments to celebrate. In November 1880, before 10,000 people, they beat Blackburn Rovers 3–0 in the Lancashire Cup Final. Suter was at fullback for the Rovers and marked Tommy Marshall. They exchanged fisticuffs, at which the spectators invaded the pitch: not the first game against Rovers at which there was crowd trouble.

Then in the second half of the season there was a last Cup run. They beat Sheffield 5–1, had a bye into the quarter-finals, paid the weak southern team Romford to travel to Darwen, and beat them 15–0 to reach the semi-final at the Oval. Their opponents were Old Carthusians, latecomers on the scene but one of the most interesting old boys teams.

One of the stronger recommendations of the Clarendon Commission of Enquiry into the Public Schools had been that Charterhouse should leave its London home, which in the seventeeth century had been on the pleasant edge of the city but was now in a workaday, slummy area. In 1872 the school moved to Godalming, and buildings surrounded by playing fields. One of the consequences was a football explosion.

The old cloisters rules had eased naturally into soccer, and at Godalming there was a vivid culture of informal training games. 'Runabout' was a lunch-time game with no limit on numbers, 'Puntabout' a kicking exercise and 'Shootabout' a goalscoring prac-tice. The main playing field was a fast narrow surface that encouraged accurate control, and the school produced a couple of generations of outstanding players, such as the Walters brothers at fullback and G. O. Smith. 'He'd eyes all round his shirt', it was said of Smith, a truly great ballplaying centre forward, who between 1893 and 1901 scored eleven goals in twenty games for England, fourteen of those games as captain.

But it was an earlier generation of brilliant Carthusians who played at the Oval on 26 March 1881, for a match that had mocking reminders of previous Darwen events.

Darwen had injuries and were weakened by the old lack of strong reserves. Nevertheless, reported *The Carthusian*, they arrived with boots 'covered in spikes and projecting studs'. Marindin was the referee, and went into the old boys' dressing room to say that this should not be allowed; but the old boys decided that it was too late to protest, and for Darwen to find new boots, although afterwards Carthusian feet and shins were badly marked.

Then the kick-off was delayed because the nineteen-year-old Carthusian J. F. M. Prinsep arrived late and eating a sandwich. A stylish halfback, he was the youngest ever England player until Wayne Rooney broke his record in 2003. While they waited for Prinsep, Darwen lined up on the field, and both the players and their many supporters shouted, 'Time! Time! Time!' When the game started Darwen scored and in a bizarre reminiscence of the Tottington match in 1830, their supporters 'sent up clouds of carrier pigeons'.

A few years before, Darwen had shocked Remnants and Old Etonians with more up-to-date tactics, but now Old Carthusians were the slicker. Twenty odd years later the football historians Gibson and Pickford described them as 'the first really scientific eleven'.

When the Carthusians equalised Darwen protested that the ball had actually gone between the upright and the guy-ropes, and when they went ahead 2–1 that the ball had been out of play. Marindin overruled both objections, Darwen became rattled, and Old Carthusians ran out 4–1 winners.

There had been a huge crowd around the *Darwen News* office, but as word came in people drifted away, and with them their dreams of glory. Old Carthusians went on to win the Cup.

Selected experts

In 1882 Blackburn Rovers reached the Cup Final but they were hampered by injuries, their own conceit and probably nerves. They overdid their passing and lost to Old Etonians. It was the last blaze of the amateur light, and at the final whistle Kinnaird did his famous hand-stand in front of the Oval pavilion. The following year Blackburn Olympic beat the Etonians 2–1 and after that it was Rovers three years in a row. They were a team of great power and skill, composed by now entirely of working-class professionals. They lined up in the 1–2–3–5 formation that would be common to soccer for the next forty years.

Old Carthusians were a definite link between this and the six-man forward lines who scrimmaged, but at the same time they were Gentlemen Amateurs. When G. O. Smith part-wrote the 'Football' volume in the Badminton Library he admitted that 'the Corinthians of my day never trained'. They kept fit by playing, as Kinnaird had done, and we might recall here that a coded accusation of professionalism often took the form of the question that N. L. Jackson asked about Blackburn Olympic: how was it that working men could afford to go away and train for a week?

The answer in Olympic's case is almost certainly

that the week was paid for by Stanley Yates, who owned an iron foundry in Birley Street. The team's player-coach, Jack Hunter, had been installed in the nearby Cotton Tree pub.

The effect of the training was that working men's health caught up somewhat with that of bigger and better fed opponents. Reports make it clear that when Blackburn Olympic beat the Etonians it was as much by stamina and energy, the way they tackled and attacked the ball, as by any superior system. An ironic twist to this situation came in 1887, when in the FA Cup sixth round Old Carthusians were beaten 2–1 by Preston North End, and in an attempt to redress the balance of skill the old boys were the first to put the boot in. Incidentally, one of the Carthusian wingers was the subsequent Hollywood film star C. Aubrey Smith.

If the Old Carthusians of 1881 nudged tactics towards something more scientific, it is most likely because they held their positions in a 1–2–2–6 formation and tried not to be drawn into scrimmages. This gave attackers a numerical advantage, of course, and the answer was to take one of the two centre forwards and put him in the middle of the halfback line. Who actually invented the 1–2–3–5 pyramid formation it is impossible to say. Historians of Turton have laid claim, but there are various other random instances. What seems certain is that some time in 1883 Preston North End made it their regular formation, and that in the same year it was employed by Cambridge University. Forwards would at last advance in line and positional specialities develop. The issue became not merely possession of the ball, but control of the space as well.

Even so, as G. O. Smith pointed out, the amateurs of the 1890s tended to use faster forward passes and attempt to outrun the fullbacks, whereas professionals 'reached goal by degrees', with passing movements that involved the whole team, and often a deeper-lying forward. This was Smith's own role, and in his England days he put the ball through for the killer striker Steve Bloomer, just as in the late 1880s the deep-lying position had been that of the Preston Invincibles' John Goodall.

In one of his books J. H. Catton, who began his journalistic career in Preston, described how 'a teacher and doctor from Glasgow' named Gledhill gave the North End players blackboard lectures on tactics, and told them how 'selected experts' might combine. Maybe there were two Dr Gledhills in Lancashire football at the same moment in history but it seems extremely unlikely, and the teacher and doctor, whether from Glasgow or not, is surely our man. And what a wonderful thing, if it was him, that what he learned in Darwen should have gone to help the creation of North End. They are the first team in whom, if we could go back in time and see them, we would find something undeniably modern. William Sudell imported them all except Fred Dewhurst and the local clergyman who kept goal, and they were brought in to fit a system, the dynamic Nick Ross at the back and the attack built around the creativity of the centre forward, John Goodall.

Sudell also displayed what is to this day the ultimate symptom of Football Mania. He embezzled his employer's money not for himself, but to finance North End. He was imprisoned, and ended his days in South Africa.

Sotheby's

Fergus Suter, the first unashamed professional, won five Lancashire Cup medals with Blackburn Rovers, and played in four FA Cup Finals, winning three times. When he moved to Blackburn he lodged in the Castle inn, Market Street Lane, and in 1883, when he was twenty-five, he married the nineteen-year-old Martha Almond, the daughter of John Almond, a cotton mill manager and a dialect writer and local dramatic critic. By the time the Football League was formed in 1888 his career was winding down and he made only one League appearance, in December 1888, when he played in goal in place of the injured regular. He enjoyed a handsome testimonial and by the 1891 Census was landlord of Blackburn's Bay Horse Hotel, which he and Martha ran with a house-keeper, a barmaid, and two boots and general men. There were no children.

Later the Suters moved to Darwen, to the Millstone and most famously the White Lion, and they retired to a house called 'Branksome', in Seafield Road, a street or two back from Blackpool Promenade. Fergus was bedridden for the last three months of his life, and died from cancer in August 1916, aged fifty-eight. It was the year that on the Somme saw the end of his world, perhaps, as well as of his life. He left an estate valued at £610 0s. 4d. When A. N. Hornby died in 1925, aged seventy-eight, having earlier fallen from a horse, he left a little over £6,000.

In August 2000 Fergus Suter's medal from the 1885 Cup Final, in which the Rovers beat West Bromwich Albion after a replay, was auctioned at Sotheby's in London. It went to an anonymous bidder for £6,500 plus the buyer's premium.

PART FOUR

Secret Chains

Play the game

In the 1870s local newspapers like the *Darwen News* and *Partick Observer* ran as part of their service to their readers syndicated romantic fiction serials, often written by women, over six or eight weekly episodes. During the period of the Old Etonian Cup ties the *Darwen News* serial was a story of true love and bigamy entitled SECRET CHAINS, OR WHICH WAS THE TRUE MARRIAGE? There is serendipity here, or at least a co-incidence, because chains were indeed forged in the heat of the Darwen adventure and its aftermath.

They are the chains which bind England's football present to its distant past. They have proved hard to shake off, and cause chafing and sores to this day. Three in particular are important. They are the mindset that deplored professionalism, the loss to football of the gentlemen amateurs, and the instincts that make Englishmen play football the way they do. All are entangled somehow with that public school notion whereby sport became a symbol, or even a substitute, for morality.

In 1913, when he was eighty, Montague Butler, the myth-making headmaster of Harrow, told a gathering which had assembled to honour him that 'there is hardly any motto that I would commend to the good friends who are sitting around me more than "Play the Game"!' Butler was a Doctor of Divinity, as well as a schoolmaster, but he did not offer the Ten Commandments, or Christ's Sermon on the Mount, or 'Give all you have to the poor and follow me.' He did not refer his good friends to the Thirty-Nine Articles of the Church of England, or to a Divine Creation to which they should adjust themselves. No. Butler advised them to Play the Game.

By which he meant what, exactly? To stick to the letter of the rules, which in all sports are subject to change? Or to stick to the spirit of the game? If the latter, what was the spirit exactly? When in his 1885 football song 'Three Yards' the Harrow master E. W. Hawson wrote that:

> They tell us the world is a scrimmage
> And life is a difficult run

who are 'they' who are telling us?

Actually, although the wisdom of the ages is implied, 'they' are Montague Butler, Dean Farrar and E. E. Bowen, making something up to justify their underlying purpose, which was to train men to run an empire, and the most famous use of the phrase 'play the game' is in Sir Henry Newbolt's poem 'Vitae Lampada'. British soldiers are in a desert war, and about to be overrun. Their surviving officer is a public school subaltern who rallies them to face death. 'Play up, play up and play the game!' But what was their war about? Markets? Raw materials? Oil?

Newbolt does not say, and the subaltern does not ask. He plays the game.

Sport as morality was a ruling-class mind-juggle, and it confused more people than it inspired. What about scugs who had no talent for sport, or aesthetes who weren't interested? Were they a lesser breed? Were women? Not to mention working-class players and spectators and men like Tom Hindle and John Lewis who were creating a new entertainment and setting a new standard of excellence. Hindle and Lewis were confused because their hearts pulled them one way and their respect for society another.

Clegg's middle way

Earlier in the nineteenth century the Liberal philos-
opher John Stuart Mill had called the Empire 'a vast
system of outdoor relief for the upper classes', but
by 1879 outdoor relief was for millworkers and the
Empire was the drama that justified everyone's existence. Men like Eccles Shorrock, Jr and the Darwen
politicos, who had fondly imagined that Free Trade
might be a universal blessing universally welcomed
without bloodshed, were out of date before they
reached the prime of their lives. And at the benefit
concert to send the Darwen team to London, middle-
class provincials who dressed up as Zulus meant no
harm beyond a topical joke, perhaps. They sang in
chapel on Sundays, after all, and had strong notions
of godliness, cleanliness and how to be good neighbours. There were always the lazy and ne'er-do-well,
and drunks like Joan Greenhalgh who smashed
windows, but Darwen was a structured world and it
seemed to have been so for ever, a cultural whole,
even when, like Harrow School traditions, it had
only been that way for about a dozen years.

   Life changes around us and we do not notice, and
by 1879 Darwen had the complete industrial landscapes, the vistas of mills that at the ends of the streets

were bulky in the damp polluted air. When I was young in the 1940s that world was still there, and still reassuring: it was finished then, of course, even though we lived in it, and it was possibly easier to inhabit than today's mishmash of entitlements, uncertainties and advert-fuelled material desires. One dwells on this because it is the essential background to the dilemmas and guilt of professionalism and the way in which a Methodist chapel-goer like J. C. Clegg was able to influence football. People like Tom Hindle and John Lewis told lies about professionalism because although it made sense they did not want to be thought disreputable. They were torn, whereas Clegg was more sure of himself and sought a middle way.

J. C. Clegg hated English class snobbery, but he did not much like working–class manners either. He was a dry, shrewd, provincial lawyer who spoke with a Sheffield accent, and on the one hand his sense of incipient abuses was correct. On the other his attitude fertilised them. If Hindle and Lewis and Clegg were alive today, Clegg would want to tell Hindle and Lewis that it was all their fault. It was their pragmatism and hypocrisy that had made inevitable the super-injunctions, the millions siphoned off by agents or trousered by unscrupulous managers, the sale of rights to photograph weddings, the divers, swearers and head-butters, and the revelations of nightclub drug girls. Inevitable, indeed, from the moment Fergus Suter sauntered through the Orchard Mill watch-house and left George Walsh's office with a few sovereigns.

Working men, Clegg would mutter in private, cannot be trusted. They don't know any better. They will always go with short-term greed. Yet the fact is that what happened after 1879 gave them little chance to find a better way.

In the fight to establish professionalism, and soccer as a spectator sport, the compelling force was once again the need for regular fixtures: in this case to provide regular income. Hence, eventually, the formation of the Football League. Before this Alcock failed several times to carry enough southern votes for the legalisation of professionalism, and in the north back-handers and subterfuge became habitual. Eventually the Lancashire clubs led by Blackburn Rovers and Preston North End threatened to form a breakaway British Football Association.

This forced the issue, in which Alcock and realists like Kinnaird and Marindin were the natural allies of the Hindles and Morleys and Sudells. But people knew then as they know today that although money had won the day it was not the only thing. Football had a meaning beyond money, and needed codes of conduct that were not determined by money. This integrity is what Clegg sought to protect. He became the single most powerful person on the FA Council, and one sees all the reasons for his authoritarian middle way, and for his notion of an impartial ruling body; but he was heavy-handed, and the events of the 1890s had mixed consequences.

The dog and its tail

From the start Clegg made life as difficult as he could for the Football League, which was at least big enough to look after itself and has always, in its original guise or as the Premiership, been the tail that more or less wags the dog. But this tension has never been productive, particularly where international football is concerned. It was all very well for Tom Hindle and his chums who were still players to vote in committee for the Lancashire FA's best eleven in 1879. That the same system was used to pick the England team until Alf Ramsey became manager in the 1960s was ludicrous, but it was a way in which the FA could assert its importance, and so they stuck with it.

And that clubs were in contention with representative bodies from the start is shown by Tom Hindle's Lancashire Football Association notes in Alcock's *Football Annual* for 1880. Prominent clubs, he complains, arranged big fixtures on what they knew to be the Lancashire Association's representative dates. *Plus ça change*.

Another Clegg policy saw him do his utmost to keep former professional players off club committees, out of boardrooms, and away from wider administration. To what extent this influenced the phenomenom of the years on either side of the First World War, when English coaches were revered in Europe but ignored at home, is hard to say. But at the very least, when we see what men like Bobby Charlton, Dave Whelan, Niall Quinn and Trevor Brooking have achieved in modern administration and boardrooms, we must think that over the years a great deal of wisdom was allowed to go to waste. Football always corrupted and exposed some people. But it has allowed many more to grow.

There is another hidden loss that dates from the 1890s, and it is that since the aftermath of the rows over professionalism men from Britain's most educated classes have had very little to do with the wider game.

The penalty kick

What is clear is that demographics doomed the Gentlemen Amateurs as surely as they doomed Darwen. As more and more people played football, public school standards were relatively lower, and families and careers and top-level sport harder to combine. It is no coincidence that a great amateur player like G. O. Smith was a schoolmaster who enjoyed long holidays. And if the Corinthians were an ideal, they also cherry-picked the best players as ruthlessly as Sudell engaged Scotsmen.

Not that the decline of the amateurs as players was the problem. The problem was the way in which they allowed themselves to be bullied and excluded, so that in many cases their resentment turned to hatred, and hatred destroyed common sense. Their first big confrontation with Clegg's FA came in 1891 over the introduction of the penalty kick. Hard-core amateurs protested against it, and for years refused to apply the law, on the grounds that no gentleman deliberately fouled an opponent in that manner. Clearly they had forgotten the sneaks who loitered offside, the admonishers who kicked them, the tackles both given and taken by an A. N. Hornby, and the general thunderclap gamesmanship of an Arthur Kinnaird.

And if a gentleman did not commit a foul he would not be punished, would he, so where was the logic in their position? It was nowhere, of course. Their objections were emotional and there was little attempt to assuage them.

The second big row was over scratch teams, which since the 1860s had been a principal feature of the game. Indeed, most early teams were scratch teams and men turned up if and when they could. It was a social custom, and adapted itself well enough to cup ties and qualification rules. Then in the late 1890s there were rumours that some amateur clubs arranged scratch games in return for a share of the gate money. It was never clear that amateurs who took gate money, if indeed any of them took it at all, did so for any other purpose than to keep their clubs afloat; which is what Darwen Rangers sought to do when in 1879 they wanted a share of the gate from their match against Darwen Reserves. Clegg's FA descended like a ton of bricks, and this was the issue over which N. L. Jackson, the founder of the Corinthians (a scratch team after all), resigned from the FA in disgust at its contempt for his opinions.

Some amateurs became so resentful that Robert Baden-Powell could write the following in his 1908 manual *Scouting for Boys*:

Football is a grand game for developing a lad physically and morally . . . But it is a vicious game when it draws crowds of lads away from playing the game themselves to be merely onlookers at a few paid performers . . . boys and young men, pale, narrow chested, hunched up, miserable specimens, smoking endless cigarettes, betting, all of them learning to be hysterical as they groan and cheer in panic unison with their neighbours . . .

In 1908 almost 75,000 people watched the Cup Final, and Englishmen abroad had already founded what became those mighty institutions AC Milan and Real Madrid. And by then the amateurs had their own Cup and their own Association, so that the gap between them and professionalism was administrative as well as emotional.

Consequences

One aspect of this stand-off was the notion within Clegg's FA that because professional football was money-damaged and morally compromised, the amateurs must be seen to be purer than pure. This led to Britain's dispute with FIFA and various foreign countries over broken-time payments, whereby amateurs received expenses for time lost at work. Sheffield footballers had been refused this in the 1860s, we may remember, although it is probable that Darwen and Blackburn employers were not above making payments in the 1870s.

In many countries soccer was not fully professional until after the Second World War, and the Swedes who won the 1948 Olympics, for example, were broken-time amateurs even if their stars then went on to Italy and earned fortunes. But for years the FA would not countenance the system. This was why for most of the 1920s it had no relations to speak of with FIFA, and for years thereafter was very frosty. The result was that it would not send England teams to the first World Cups after 1930. Decades of tactical thinking and experience passed England by. Most of us would agree, one guesses, that as events turned out this was not a good thing.

Again, while J. C. Clegg objected to the subterfuges and smart-aleck tricks that became endemic to English football, others might say that illegal deals became inbred because it was impossible to discuss financial matters with true openness. For years football was an entertainment business with turnover but few reserves of cash, and it was regulated to keep smaller clubs in existence. That is the reason for the retain and transfer system (denounced by Clegg as 'slavery') and the imposition of a maximum wage in 1901. This was never fair on crowd-pulling stars, and until the 1960s players like Suter with his 'personal reasons' broke the rules to get a share of what they were worth.

Suppose the educated, sophisticated and on the whole generous realism of men like Alcock, Kinnaird and Marindin had continued to be dominant in the Football Association, and that people of the gentleman amateur type had been more involved in the board-rooms of professional clubs. Would the game's ambience have been different and some of its hypocrisies avoided? It is impossible to say, but it is interesting to remember how the Cobbold family ran Ipswich Town during the regimes of Alf Ramsey and Bobby Robson, and that at Arsenal the Bracewell-Smiths presided over many decades of stability and success.

Kinnaird did stay on as a figurehead, of course, and J. H. Catton was to write in 1920 that for all Alcock's qualities football grew too big for him. He had resigned the secretaryship of the FA in 1895, pleading pressure of his other work. Something left with him, one feels, and has never been replaced.

Perhaps the truth is that football's divisions reflected those of our class-ridden country when it ruled the world, and, as we know, we are still stuck with many of them, in both life and football.

Smash, dash and at 'em

There is a final secret chain that binds us to the Darwen and Old Etonian past, and it is perhaps the most intriguing. This is the instinctive nature of the English game, and the unconscious habits and impulses of its men as they run on to the field to play.

English footballers are widely regarded as unskilled compared to many foreigners, and the long ball and the kick and rush are seen to this day as the essence of the English game. And the fact is, of course, that they are. A tension between the primitive and the skilful has driven English football since the 1830s at least, and the long ball and the rush describe what the game was like when folk football became, say, the Eton Field Game. When the Etonian Robin Lubbock said that his Field Game tactic was 'smash, dash and at 'em' he articulated a race memory of folk football, and the very spirit of bolshiness in the English character that in Darwen chased a ball from near Blackburn to halfway up the moors.

Such things are deep. They are deep instincts in the players and deep desires for action in the spectators, and if we ask what it is that has made the Premiership the world's top TV sporting attraction, so that boys in African villages with no running water sport shirts which say ROONEY or TORRES, and millions tune in every week, it is this age-old drama that they want.

Attack like Tottington when the pigeons were thrown up. Go forward. Smash, dash and at 'em. Talk about Russians and Bashi-Bazouks, they weren't in it. Long throw-ins for Stoke City are as long as Kinnaird's must have been with the wind behind them at the Oval, and every bit as annoying. Are you ready, said Alcock as he looked around the field before the kick-off, and the world has said yes, we're ready, from forgotten Bromley Cross to Kuala Lumpur and distant Beijing, and the shores of that ocean into which, from beneath a White Ensign, Jimmy Love's body was decanted.

What is wrong with English football is what it cannot help being, and what has made it endlessly popular. And no matter how much our football frustrates us, we cannot deny that sport, as a recreation and a spectator entertainment, and as a lesson in life to young people, was Victorian England's greatest gift to civilisation; or that the singing from behind the goal, which is gutter filth at worst, is at best a lullaby for all that is broken in the world, but that the beautiful game can put together for a moment. O my Suter and my Kirkham long ago!

Extras

Manchester Central Library
I like a few extras in the manner of a DVD release. People don't have to view or read them, and they have no place in the actual work, but they say things that have been crucial to the film director or writer or whoever. In my case I became interested in the early history of football in the 1950s, when I was working in a cotton mill and before I got a job on a newspaper. I would go to the domed reading room of the Manchester Central Library and pore over Edwardian volumes like Gibson and Pickford's *Association Football and the Men Who Made It*.

Such books are redolent of their era: ivory gloss paper, decorated chapter headings, stately photographs, some protected by tissue paper, and coloured images of players tooled into the thick board covers make them delectable objects to this day. Within, the prose is sonorous, and the desire to make soccer seem respectable is very strong. Of scandal there is not a whiff, of William Sudell's imprisonment for stealing money to buy players not a mention.

Football in Gibson and Pickford is all heroic, and perhaps that is why the story of Darwen versus Old Etonians leaps from their pages, and has fascinated me since I first read it therein. Over the next half-century I made several attempts to write about it, and have finally managed to do so in this book.

Writing is a long game, really, and never proceeds as one thinks it will. Bottom drawers contain failures, dead ends and lost dreams, but sometimes these recur at their rightful time, as this subject matter has for me. There was something about it that I could not work through until now, and I guess that it was my sense of the lost world of the cotton towns, and of how people were around 1879. That time has never seemed distant to me because of the people I loved who were alive in it.

My people in 1879

My grandparents were teenagers in 1879. They all lived to be eighty or more. I knew them well, and they throw light upon the cotton town people and attitudes described in this book. My paternal grandfather, Fred Dewhurst, died in 1953 aged eighty-nine and in his last months would talk to me about his grandmother. She was a tall, thin, red-haired woman named Olive Crabtree, and in her turn she had told him about the most exciting event of her girlhood.

Her family were handloom weavers with a small-holding on the moors above Todmorden, and it was an early summer evening, when the fading light and dewy humidity up there can still be magical. There are small flowers that gleam, and an odd, breathless, gentle, almost visible silence in which close sounds are muffled and far ones carry. One of the women had taken her spinning-wheel outside and the men smoked their pipes.

Then they heard shouts and saw a man waving his arms as he ran across the moor. They recognised him as a neighbour who lived about half a mile away, and when he reached them he recovered his breath and told them his great news: Wellington had beaten Bonaparte at Waterloo, and the Wars were over.

Thirty years later, as the handloom weaving collapsed, Olive Crabtree's husband was a Chartist who kept a musket up the chimney, and soon after they abandoned the moors and went down to the valley and Todmorden to find work. They could read and write and were used to the stripping down and maintenance of machinery, and Olive's son, my great-grandfather Joseph, became an overlooker in a power mill. My grandfather was sent to a Dame School, and remembered pissing into the River Calder that ran at the back of the building. When he was eight he went into the mill with his father, as what he called a beamer: he crawled under the looms to attach the threads.

Then came the slump of 1878, which caused riots in Darwen and drove Suter south. My grandfather lost his job. He was thirteen and tramped down the Rossendale Valley towards Blackburn to look for work. He slept rough and one day, on the edge of Blackburn, he sat by the road and wept. A woman came out of her house and gave him a glass of water. She said that there wasn't any work, that his mother would be worried about him, and that he should go home; which he did.

He remembered the frost at the beginning of 1879 and that later in the year trade picked up. My great-grandfather gave up his job, at which the weavers in Lord Brother's shed presented him with an ornamental clock, and moved the family to Oldham. He became an under-manager at the Derker Mill, in the middle of the town, and my grandfather, after night school and much diligence, became a technical expert and a self-made, late-Victorian cotton patriarch.

For a time he rented an entire mill but lost it in another slump and was snapped up for his expertise by the Oldham Velvet Company. In his heyday he would punch out a jacquard pattern for one dress length of cut velvet for my grandmother (real velvet, not the velveteen that is called velvet today) and he progressed from manager to managing director and chairman.

His younger brother, John, who died before I was born, became the private secretary and man of confidence to one of the last of the old-style Oldham mill owners. John had a Rolls-Royce and lived alone, looked after by a chauffeur named Griffiths, who wore a cross-buttoned uniform jacket and gaiters. Were they a gay couple? More than likely, although of course such things did not happen in those days.

Both great-uncle John and my grandfather bought and sold mill shares, and my grandfather lost a fortune in the 1929 crash. But he was always comfortably off, and chairman of the board until the end. He liked cricket and rugby league, and soccer was not really his game, although he had a ticket to the first Wembley Cup Final in 1923. He could not get in because of the crush, but he was staying at the same hotel as the victorious Bolton Wanderers, and that night got to drink out of the Cup.

In 1953 we watched England regain the Ashes on TV together, and when he shuffled back from the lavatory I had to button his flies for him because his fingers were too arthritic.

He read Shakespeare and dialect poets like Samuel Laycock and John Critchley Prince, and would always talk about what he called 'leafy England' – not a description of our moors, or of anywhere he ever lived, actually. An England of the broken heart, I suppose. Not that he was nostalgic. He was hard and forward-looking, and had stood in the Velvet Company's Falcon Mill watch-house to shut the gates on latecomers.

He contained in himself both the out-of-work operatives in Darwen and the mill owners who laid them off. When he was laid off himself he stood the losses. He believed in self-help and unlike my grand-mother he had little sense of humour; perhaps hers, which was riotous, had been what attracted him, because he loved her very much. He was selfish, but he knew that Lancashire cotton was one of history's epics.

My mother's father, Teddy Carter, showed the other side of a Victorian coin. He had been a compositor and staunch union man on the *Manchester Guardian* when print shops were still radical hot-beds, and became a Lloyd George Liberal. He lived in Chadderton, contiguous to Oldham, where Liberals controlled the Council and found him a job as Registrar of Births,

Marriages and Deaths. This meant that in effect he could be a full-time local politician. He was a councillor, a magistrate and for many years chairman of the Education Committee. I still have the ceremonial trowel with which he laid the cornerstone of the North Chadderton Senior Elementary School. At the end of his life he was blind, and would play me at dominoes by touch.

His son survived Gallipoli, was in cotton and reached the boardroom of one of the last combines put together by the banks after the slump of the 1930s; all gone now, of course. His daughters, my Auntie Doris and my mother, became elementary school teachers. One of Auntie Doris's friends, whom I met in the 50s, was a woman named Annie Gledhill: whether she was the niece of the unmarried doctor who in 1891 lived round the corner with his brother and sister I do not know. Gledhill is a Yorkshire name, I believe.

Neither of my grandmothers worked, nor my unmarried aunt Olive Dewhurst, because women not working was a sign of middle-class success. Grandma Constance Carter was the daughter of a blacksmith, and a bit like Nancy Hindle in Darwen, because one of her family had married into the fag end of a mill-owning dynasty; thus at second or third remove Constance knew women who went to Paris to buy furniture. It shocked her, if anything, because she was unassuming. The Carter household had a female relative with them, known as Little Auntie, who played the piano as well as doing all the cooking.

Auntie Doris married a schoolmaster. They were interested in books and the theatre. Once all these people went to Chapel every Sunday but now they didn't: the Great War had intervened.

Grandma Emma Jane Dewhurst was snappy-capable, and a marvellous cook of traditional fare such as hotpots, steak and kidney puddings, trimmings and stuffings for birds, and puddings, cakes and jam tarts and so forth. Her back kitchen contained a range and the furniture which had been their best when they were first married, and she would shell peas into a bowl in her lap and give vigorous instructions to my aunt, who was at the actual stove (by now electric) in the adjoining scullery. Grandma always wore a black velvet choker and had a cheerful but bossy way with tradesmen. She read modern novels but never talked about them, and kept the ones with sex scenes in a bedroom drawer. She deployed ill-health to get her way, wrapped her prejudices in deadly observations and was straitlaced with a rebel's laugh. When she was composed she was upright and handsome, and yet once, in a public park in the late 30s, I saw her turn like a vixen and drive away a beggar woman and her unwashed children. Get away. Get off, you bitch. You're a filthy disgrace.

That was an authentic voice, I guess, if a chilling one: the voice of cotton town respectability when she was a teenage girl awakening to choices, in about 1879.

Sudell's playmaker
In 1956 I was working on the Manchester *Evening Chronicle* and for two weeks assembled the 'Northern

Window' social column when the regular compiler, Fred Isaac, a big bluff man with charm and a moustache, was off sick. One day an elderly man came in seeking publicity: he was the advance road manager for the German magician Kalanag, whose show was due at the Ardwick Empire the following week. Kalanag's master trick was to bring a Mercedes-Benz on stage, sit a girl on the bonnet, and at the flick of a finger make both disappear. After his death rumours spread that Kalanag had stolen the tricks of persecuted Jewish magicians, and later used his stage equipment to smuggle money to exiled Nazis in South America. But in 1956 he still warranted friendly publicity.

His mission accomplished, my elderly visitor chatted and told me that he had not been to Manchester for many years, although he was born nearby.

'Where?' I said.

'Glossop,' he replied.

The town halfway up the moors between Manchester and Sheffield. In the early 1900s its football team was in the First Division. Did I know that? I did.

'I played for them,' said the elderly man.

'Did you know John Goodall?' I said.

He did.

Goodall: the legend; playmaker of Sudell's Preston North End Cup and League double team, later of Derby County and, for a twilight year or two, Glossop.

'What was he like?' I said.

'He did this amazing thing,' said the old boy. 'He dribbled the ball with the inside of his heel.'

Golly, I thought. Amazing indeed.

Some fifty years later I was invited by Angus Graham-Campbell to watch the Field Game at Eton, and the first thing I saw was a fifteen-year-old boy dribbling the ball up the by-line with the inside of his heel. It was a trick of the Eton football, to get the ricochet and the rouge, and Goodall must have picked it up somewhere and preserved it, because even in the soccer of around 1910 it was a freak survival; although still going on in the Field Game.

Then while writing this book I have been made to think about that other, earlier centre forward James Gledhill, who played against the Old Etonians at the Oval, and maybe gave the blackboard lectures to Preston North End when Goodall was William Sudell's playmaker. Did Gledhill see Goodhart and Whitfeld bring the ball up that way, or shield it that way and then turn, and did he try it himself and then pass on the idea? Or did all sorts of people always do it, until harder tacklers and markers, and a faster tempo, forced a change?

Who knows? The past is lost for ever, and yet it is never as distant as we think, and its secret chains attach us to our humanity.

Swagger

Because of the way in which the staff came to involve themselves in Harrow sports, and the moment at which they did so, Footer has had a more obvious effect upon general British culture than the Eton Field Game, even though the Field Game displays the ideals of an elite in a more profound and moving way. In the first place there is the word Footer itself. That posh English slang whereby '-er' is added to the ends of words is supposed to have been invented at Harrow, and Footer to have been one of its earliest coinings. Christopher Tyerman, the historian of Harrow, gives as the extreme example of this lingo 'wagger pagger bagger', for wastepaper basket, and 'Thicker', for the Ancient Greek historian Thucydides, is another classic.

'Swagger' related to particulars of dress, and some Houses even printed their own Swagger Rules. 'Buck up', on all our lips at one time or another, is pure Footer speak. It was shouted at men to make them play harder. On the other hand 'lockers', for the hours spent after the boarding houses locked up for the night, was in use at Captain Markham's Westminster, so maybe these things are airborne and contagious.

Charles Costeker and Billy the Kid

This last Extra is about non-football documents in the Singleton Collection. The catalogue for the 1878 auction in which their grandfather's school premises were bought and sold had obvious family interest, and the boys also saved the 1875 prospectus when Gregson's Carrs Mill was floated on the Stock Exchange at a nominal value of £30,000 in £5 shares. The Gregsons were retiring to Southport, but were on the board of the new Darwen Cotton Manufacturing Company, as was their former mill manager. Charles Costeker was the company's solicitor.

Since the Gregson's Mill mentioned in the report of the 1879 Relief Fund is that of the Darwen

Company, and it was the boys who kept the report, we might surmise that a member of the family had either worked in the mill or bought shares. People often did both, my grandfather, father and uncles among them.

A later document, which also emphasises how in a small town a solicitor like Charles Costeker could have a finger in every pie, is the most intriguing.

This is an 1885 prospectus for the Omaha Cattle Company Ltd, seeking to raise £100,000 in a thousand £10 shares to lease almost half a million acres of unoccupied US Government land in New Mexico and ranch cattle. Charles Huntington and J. G. Potter, the Darwen wallpaper men, were the directors, and Costeker and a London firm the company's solicitors.

This is interesting as an example of how English and Scots capital was invested in the American West, and because from 1865 to 1900 New Mexico and Arizona were the scene of bitter conflicts between railroads and capitalist enterprises on the one side and small settlers and townspeople on the other. Persons involved in those conflicts became legends of Wild West mythology: Billy the Kid, Pat Garrett, the Earp brothers and Doc Holliday.

The Republican big-business Governor of New Mexico was Lew Wallace, ex-Union Army General and the future writer of the novel *Ben Hur*, and the Lincoln County War of 1878 was a struggle between two capitalist interests, one of them financed from London by a young English businessman named Tunstall. Tunstall hired Billy the Kid as a ranch-hand

and eventually a soldier in the war. Tunstall and his American partner were killed, and although Billy the Kid was promised a pardon Governor Wallace reneged. Pat Garrett was sent to find Billy, and did so at Fort Sumner, where he killed him with a single shot in the middle of the night, four months after Darwen played Old Carthusians.

The Colfex County War against the Maxwell Land Grant Company, a huge empire whose power lasted until the 1960s, began in the early 1870s and spluttered across northern New Mexico, where the Omaha Company had its grant, until about 1900. A small rancher named Clay Allison was the notable resistance gunfighter.

In Arizona the Earps were Republicans who invested their frontier bordello and gambling saloon profits in capitalist mining ventures, which they helped to defend against smallholders, and petty ranchers and rustlers. Some of the smaller people were earlier Hispanic settlers, but most were poor whites voting Democrat who had migrated from older Southern states. In this way class, racial and Civil War conflicts continued.

An obituary of J. G. Potter said that the Omaha Cattle Company was not a good investment. Maybe the land itself was not good enough, or refrigerated meat from South America changed the market, or the semi-lawlessness of New Mexico made business too difficult to conduct at a distance. Tunstall did after all go in person to Lincoln County.

How economic power defined events in the West is what Michael Cimino tried to dramatise in his confused movie epic *Heaven's Gate*, and is sketchily present in the back plot of Sam Peckinpah's wonderfully elegiac *Pat Garrett and Billy the Kid*. And old Sam and his disputes with the Hollywood studios are after all a vivid modern version of the little man in his struggle against corporate power.

Such agreeable digressions aside, it is interesting that little Darwen had connections to two of modern popular culture's most potent myths: that of the Wild West, and that of every footballer, football team and supporter, the Dream of the Frontier, and the Dream of the Game. Neither of them, as we know, are unsullied.

Acknowledgements

Many people have enabled this book to be written and I must thank Matt Phillips, Rachel Cugnoni, Susannah Otter and Matt Broughton at Yellow Jersey, copy editor Mark Handsley, Tristan Jones, Gordon Wise at Curtis Brown, Edward Hall, my friend the film editor George Akers, who trawled the internet, Emma Dewhurst, who did the word processing, John Salthouse, who chatted football, Angus Graham-Campbell, Alexandra Cann and Jo Evans.

Librarians have been marvellous: Graham Groom, Mary Painter and their colleagues at Darwen, David Barber at the Football Association, Richard McBrearty and his colleagues at the Scottish Football Museum, Jo Miller at Surrey County Cricket Club, Penny Hatfield at the Eton College Archive, Rita Boswell, archivist at both Harrow and Westminster Schools, James Virgin of the Harrow Association, Paula Moorhouse at the Manchester Central Library, the Elders at the Mormon Family History Centre in London and staff at the Blackburn Library, the Mitchell Library, Glasgow, the Charterhouse Archive and bookshop, and the British Library Newspaper Archive at Colindale. I must also thank Joanna Lavelle,

Foundation Director at Queen Elizabeth's Grammar School Blackburn, and her colleagues.

Angus Graham-Campbell, whose collection of books about Eton is as splendid as his conversation, invited me to the Field Game, in particular one in which he team-managed a scratch side of old boys to victory with mind games in the tradition of Arthur Kinnaird, and which would not have disgraced Sir Alex Ferguson. Henry Hely-Hutchinson provided a droll touchline commentary on these events; except that he was not sure that Etonians call it the touchline.

Bibliography

Books etc. that I have consulted I will list under subject headings.

Darwen
Aspden, R. A., The Duxbury Family of Over Darwen, 1990
Barratt's Darwen Directory, 1878
Blackburn Standard, 1872
Breeze, Paul, *Darwen Football Club Memories*, Posh Up North, 1995
Darwen News, 1876ff
Doyle, Margaret Stevenson, *Social Control in Over Darwen, Lancashire,* a dissertation submitted in partial fulfilment of the degree of MA, University of Lancaster, 1972
East Lancashire Cricket and Football Times, 1879
Lewis, Richard, *Death in the Peaceful Valley: The Demise of Darwen Football Club 1885–1899, Transactions of the Historical Society of Lancashire and Cheshire*, 1995
Marshall, Julian Malim, *Eccles Shorrock (1827–89): His Biography*, Master of Philosophy Dissertation for the Faculty of Arts, University of Southampton, 1994
Obituaries files and cuttings books, Darwen Public Library
Shaw, J. G., *Darwen and Its People*, 1889, reprinted 1991
Swain, Peter, *Cultural Continuity and Football in Nineteenth Century Lancashire,* Routledge, 2008
Twydell, Dave, *Rejected F.C.,*Vol. 2, Harefield, 1995

Turton
Peet, Jack, *Who Wants a Game?*, Friends of Turton Tower

Bibliography

Blackburn

Delaney, Terence, *A Century of Soccer*, W. Heinemann/FA, 1963

Francis, Charles, *The History of Blackburn Rovers, 1875–1925*, reprinted Soccer Books, 2001

Kay, Harry, *Things about Blackburn Rovers*, J. Dickinson and Sons, 1949

Jackman, Mike, *Blackbun Rovers: A Complete Record, 1875–1990*, Breedon Books, 1990

Early cotton industry, etc.

Aiken, John, *A Description of the Country from Thirty to Forty Miles round Manchester*, 1795, reprinted

Aspin, Chris, *The Water Spinners*, Helmshore Local History Society, 2003

Begley, J. J., *A History of Lancashire*, Phillimore, 1956

Rose, Mary B. (ed.), *The Lancashire Cotton Industry: A History since* 1700, Lancashire County Books, 1996

Rothwell, M., *Industrial Heritage*, M. Rothwell, 1979

Victorian and Edwardian Manchester and East Lancashire from Old Photographs, Batsford, 1974

General football history

Alcock, Charles (ed.), *Football Annual*, 1872 ff.

Catton, J. H., *The Real Football*, Alfred Henry, 1900

—, *The Story of Association Football*, 1926, reprinted Soccer Books, 2006

Cavallini, Rob, *The Wanderers F.C.*, Dog and Duck, 2005

Gibson and Pickford, *Association Football and the Men Who Made It*, Caxton, 1905

Green, Geoffrey, *History of the Football Association*, Naldrett Press, 1953

Mason, Tony, *Association Football and English Society*, Harvester, 1980

Sanders, Richard, *Beastly Fury*, Bantam, 2009

Sutcliffe, C. E. and F. Hargreaves, *The History of the Lancashire Football Association*, Geo. Toulmin and Sons, 1928

Eton College
An Old Etonian (Henry Blake), *Reminiscences of Eton*, 1831
Coleridge, Gilbert, *Eton in the Seventies*, Smith, Elder & Co., 1912
Doraime, James, *The Eton Game*, 1902
The Eton Field Book 1869–79
Gambier-Parry, Major (ed.), *Annals of an Eton House*, J. Murray, 1907
Titchenor-Darrell, Robert, *Eton and Harrow Past and Present at Lord's*, 1996

Harrow School
The Harrow Almanack, 1865 ff.
The Harrow School Register 1800–1911, Longmans Green, 1911
Harrow Sixth Form Match Book, 1866 ff.
Howson, Edward W. and George Townsend Warner (eds), *Harrow School*, Edward Arnold, 1898
Tyerman, Christopher, *A History of Harrow School*, Oxford University Press, 2000

Westminster School
The Elizabethan, 1847
Forshall, Frederick H., *Westminster School Past and Present*, Wyman & Sons, 1884
Markham, Captain F., *Recollections of a Town Boy at Westminster*, Edward Arnold, 1903
Sargeaunt, John, *Annals of Westminster School*, Methuen, 1898

Charterhouse
Bailey, Michael, *From Cloisters to Cup Finals*, JJG Publishing, 2009

Scotland
Archer, Jan, *The Jags: The Century History of Partick Thistle Football Club*, Molendinar Press, 1976
Partick Observer, September 1876 ff.
Partick Thistle F.C.: The Official History, Harefield, 2002
Partick Thistle: The People's Club, Mary Hill Community Central Hall, Woodside and North Kelvin Local History Project

Bibliography

Robinson, Richard, *History of the Queen's Park Football Club*, Hay Nisbet & Co., 1920

Scottish Association Football Annual, 1876 ff.

Miscellaneous

Alverstone, R. E. W., and C. W. Alcock (eds), *Surrey Cricket*, Longmans Green, 1902

Cannadine, David, *Aspects of Aristocracy*, Yale University Press, 1994

Dictionary of National Biography

Illustrated London News, 1878 and 1879

Milner, Clyde A., Carol A. O'Connor and Martha A. Sandweiss (eds), *The Oxford History of the American West*, Oxford University Press, 1994

Trades Union Commission, *The Sheffield Outrages*, Adams and Dart, 1971

G.M. Young (ed.), *Early Victorian England*, Oxford University Press, 1931

Index

Index

formations 96

goalkeepers 94, 184

headers 194

line-ups 94, 254–5

offside law 25–6, 40, 96, 184

penalty kick 269–71

professionalism in 213, 239–42, 243–5, 254, 256, 268

public school development of 17–19, 20–7

residential qualifications 213

retain and transfer system 273

ruthlessness in 115

scratch teams 270

training 208–10, 254–6

trundler-in 15, 25

wages 243–5

Football Annual 78, 88, 169, 178, 208, 267

Football Association Committee 194

Football Association Cup Competition 2, 75, 82, 103–4, 106, 111, 126, 148, 150, 167, 170, 173–4, 179, 189, 194, 218, 229, 237, 248, 255, 271

Football Association (FA) 17, 32, 38–40, 66, 88, 92, 111, 165, 171, 177, 213, 223, 273

Football League 148, 257, 266, 267

Football Mania 3, 127, 133, 191, 221, 236–8, 249, 256

Forest FC (*later* Wanderers FC) 39, 170

Forshall, Frederick 24

French (Remnants defender) 173

Frere, Sir Bartle 197–8

Gambier-Parry, Major, *Annals of an Eton House* 187, 188, 190–1

Gangforward club 89

Gardner, Hugh 91

Garrett, Pat 287–8

Gentlemen Amateurs 17, 25, 166, 177, 178, 208, 269–71

George inn 32

Gibson, Alfred 253, 277–8

Gilby (groundsman at Harrow) 56

Gitanos FC 178, 179

Gladstone, Herbert 188

Gladstone, William 42, 61–3, 64, 228

Glasgow Academicals 87

Glasgow Charity Cup 145

Glasgow Deaf and Dumb Institute 86

Glasgow Herald 88, 94, 99

Glasgow Public Parks Cup Competition 89

Glasgow Rangers 88, 139, 230

Glasgow shipyards 97–8

Glasgow YMCA 86, 87

Gledhill, Dr James

  description of 142, 169

  football debut 143–4

  gives lectures to Preston North End 256

  misses a match anecdote 149, 219

  represents Lancashire FA 207, 222

  style and position of play 142, 146, 147, 150, 151, 152, 172, 204, 205, 206, 214, 215, 216

  thoughts concerning 285

Glencoe FC 89, 111

Gloag, John 103

Goodall, John 256, 284–5

Goodall, Mr 159

Goodhart, H.C. 179, 202, 203, 205, 215, 221

Govan 85

Govan Poor Relief 97

Govan Union 89

Grace, W.G. 171, 242

Graham, Jane (d.1867) 63, 64

Graham, John 17–18

Graham, Reverend Philip (b.1822) 63–4, 129, 130, 131, 133, 134, 202

Graham-Campbell, Angus 285

Grantham FC 82, 83

Great Harwood 131

Greenhalgh, Joan 213, 264

Greenway Arms (Darwen) 79, 111, 234

Greenway, Reverend Charles 64, 134

Greenway family 12, 33, 64

Greenwood, 'Doc' 227, 228

Gregson family 286

Grenadier Guards 193

Grey Horse Inn 14

Haileybury School 45

Hall, Josiah 159

Hallam 106

Halliwell, James 158

Hargreaves, Fred 227, 228

301

Index